The
Upward
Spiral

Using Neuroscience to
Reverse the Course of Depression,
One Small Change at a Time

ALEX KORB, PhD

New Harbinger Publications, Inc.

T0019173

Publisher's Note

This publication is designed to provide accurate and authoritative information in regard to the subject matter covered. It is sold with the understanding that the publisher is not engaged in rendering psychological, financial, legal, or other professional services. If expert assistance or counseling is needed, the services of a competent professional should be sought.

NEW HARBINGER PUBLICATIONS is a registered trademark of
New Harbinger Publications, Inc.

Distributed in Canada by Raincoast Books

Copyright © 2015 by Alex Korb
          New Harbinger Publications, Inc.
          5674 Shattuck Avenue
          Oakland, CA 94609
          www.newharbinger.com

Parts of this book first appeared, in different form, on the author's *Psychology Today* blog.

Cover design by Amy Shoup
Text design by Michele Waters-Kermes
Acquired by Angela Autry Gorden
Edited by Jennifer Eastman

All Rights Reserved

Library of Congress Cataloging-in-Publication Data on file

Printed in the United States of America

FSC
www.fsc.org
MIX
Paper from
responsible sources
FSC® C011935

24   23   22

20   19   18   17   16

"Alex Korb's *The Upward Spiral* is a masterful account of the neuroscience behind depression, as well as of concrete steps that will lead to an 'upward spiral' out of depression. Korb explains neuroscience in a clear and accessible way, and shows how various brain malfunctions lead to different symptoms of depression.... Throughout the [book], Korb circles back to some of his own experiences, making his account all the more powerful and real. This book is a must-read for those who struggle with depression and want some guidance on how to understand and manage it—as well as for therapists who want to learn more about the neuroscience of depression and its treatment."

>—**Elyn Saks**, Orrin B. Evans Professor of law, psychology, psychiatry, and the behavioral sciences at the University of Southern California Gould School of Law, and author of *The Center Cannot Hold*

"Alex Korb's *The Upward Spiral* is a clear and engaging explanation of the neuroscience behind depression. Korb sheds light on this mysterious and often misunderstood disorder, and, in the process, enlightens the reader about the basics of the brain and how it shapes—and is shaped by—our moods, motivations, decisions, and actions."

>—**Anson Dorrance**, head coach of the UNC-Chapel Hill Women's Soccer team and coauthor of *The Vision of a Champion*

"*The Upward Spiral* presents an engaging, accessible, and informative synthesis of the current thinking on depression and its treatment. A cohesive neuroscience perspective is skillfully interwoven with a practical guide to strategies that can both attenuate pathological negative moods, as well as enhance emotional well-being across the clinical spectrum."

>—**Helen S. Mayberg**, professor of psychiatry in neurology and radiology, and Dorothy C. Fuqua Chair in psychiatric neuroimaging and therapeutics at Emory University School of Medicine

For Mandy and all the girls she left behind

Contents

Foreword   vii

Introduction   1

Part 1: Stuck in a Downward Spiral

1   A Brain Map of Depression   9

2   Trapped with Anxiety and Worry   33

3   Always Noticing the Negative   47

4   Caught in Bad Habits   63

Part 2: Creating an Upward Spiral

5   Exercise Your Brain   77

6   Set Goals, Make Decisions   93

7   Give Your Brain a Rest   107

8   Develop Positive Habits   123

9   Take Advantage of Biofeedback   137

10   Activate a Gratitude Circuit   151

11   Rely on the Power of Others   161

12   Your Brain in Therapy   179

Conclusion   193

Acknowledgments   197

Notes   199

Foreword

In this marvelous tour of the brain, our able guide Alex Korb offers us practical knowledge and useful tools that can help us improve our lives from the very first pages—from different ways of thinking to specific actions we can take. But how can knowledge and tools actually help us?

We now know that what you do with your mind—how you focus your attention, intentionally shape your thoughts, and purposefully calm your emotions—can directly change your brain. That's the key to *neuroplasticity*—how our experiences, including what we do with our minds, actually change the activity and even the lifelong remodeling of our brains. As a practicing psychiatrist, I've learned that knowing about the details of how the brain works can uniquely empower people to improve their lives. This book offers powerful and practical ways you can use this neural knowledge to enhance your relationships, decrease worry and anxiety, and lessen the burden of depressive thinking and moods.

In this engaging immersion, you'll enter the important world of applied neuroscience with someone whose doctoral work at one of the most prestigious neuroscience programs in the world, as well as his own personal journey, has brought him up close and personal with the ability of the human brain to right itself from its unfortunate tendency to spiral downward into worry, anxiety, and depression. Whether you or someone you know is prone to excessive ruminations, self-deprecating inner commentaries, or outright depressive moods, or you simply want to enhance your life by using incisive knowledge about your brain to make life more understandable and enjoyable, this book will be a gift along your journey.

The Upward Spiral has been a joy for me in its clarity, its cutting-edge science, and its inspiring translation of current research into practical tools for everyday life. Even though this is my field as a neuropsychiatrist, psychotherapist, and mental-health educator who focuses on the brain, I learned a ton and laughed a lot. This book is at the same time informative and fun.

I am happy and honored to offer these first words of welcome to you as you learn how the various regions of your brain can come to work well together to contribute to lessening your worry and enhancing your well-being. You can turn a tendency toward a downward spiral of depression and anxiety into an upward spiral of joy and clarity in your life. Amazingly, science now affirms that you can use your knowledge and understanding to change the way you harness the power of your mind to create wellness, joy, and connection in your life. And this book will show you how.

—Daniel J. Siegel, MD

Introduction

In Madison, Wisconsin, a woman in her early thirties sits with her husband in a waiting room filling out paperwork. A scientist calmly attaches electrodes to her ankle, then leads her to an MRI machine. The MRI begins clicking and buzzing loudly, recording her brain activity as a small screen alerts her to impending electric shocks. While she's lying there dreading the coming sting, a predictable set of brain regions lights up, mostly in the circuits responsible for worrying and discomfort.[1] Later, they scan her again, this time while her husband holds her hand. She still gets the same shocks and the same warnings, but her brain response has changed. The activity in both the worrying and discomfort circuits calms down.

In Japan, a young man pedals a stationary bike as scientists use infrared light sensors to monitor the blood flow in his brain. Just fifteen minutes of biking is sufficient to increase activity in circuits responsible for emotional control and to raise levels of the neurotransmitter serotonin.[2]

In a hospital in Pittsburgh, as patients recover from spinal surgery, doctors measure the amount of sunlight in each room. They find that the patients moved to sunny rooms suddenly have a higher tolerance for pain and need less medication.[3]

These studies hint at our new understanding of the neuroscience of depression. Neuroscience is the study of the brain, including the biological basis behind our thoughts, feelings, and actions.

Research in the last few decades has dramatically changed our view of the brain circuits that cause depression and increased our knowledge of what you can do about it.

Essentially, your brain is full of intricate, interacting neural circuits. There's a worrying circuit and a habit circuit. There's a decision-making circuit and a pain circuit. There are circuits for sleep, memory, mood, planning, enjoyment, and more, and they all communicate with each other. We've all got the same circuits, whether you have depression or not, though the specific tuning of each circuit varies from person to person. The disease of depression is a pattern of activity that arises from the interactions of all these circuits. While that might not sound like much, the effects can be devastating.

Sometimes everything just feels difficult and pointless. It's a feeling we all get from time to time, and it's simply a natural by-product of our complex brain circuitry. And for most people, it's just a fleeting feeling, gone like a whisper. But due to slight differences in neurobiology, some people get stuck.

Fortunately, the studies described above—and dozens of others—beautifully illustrate how small life changes actually change the activity and chemistry in specific circuits. We know the circuits that contribute to depression, and we know how to modify those circuits. As brain activity and chemistry begin to change, so does the course of depression.

Depression Is a Downward Spiral

We all know what it means to be stuck in a downward spiral. Maybe one Friday night you're invited to a party, but you have a brief thought like *I don't think it'll be that fun,* so you don't go. Instead, you stay up too late on the couch watching television. The next day you sleep in and don't have much energy. No one calls you, so you feel even more isolated, and now you're even less likely to be social. Nothing seems particularly interesting, so you just lie around all weekend. Pretty soon you're unhappy and alone, and you don't know what you can do about it, because every decision feels wrong. This is the edge of what it means to be depressed.

Downward spirals occur because the events that happen to you and the decisions you make change your brain activity. If your brain activity changes for the worse, it contributes to everything snowballing out of control, which further exacerbates your negative brain changes, and so on. Fortunately, for most people, the activity in various brain circuits allows them to stop and reverse the downward spiral. But others aren't so lucky.

People often think depression is just being sad all the time, but it's far more than that. In fact, people with depression do not necessarily feel sad—they often feel numb, like an emptiness where emotion should be. Hopeless and helpless. Things that used to be enjoyable aren't fun anymore: food, friends, hobbies. Energy plummets. Everything feels difficult, and it's hard to explain why, because it shouldn't be. Nothing seems worth the effort it requires. It's hard to fall asleep and to stay asleep. Aches and pains are felt more deeply. It's hard to concentrate, and you feel anxious, ashamed, and alone.

The big problem with the downward spiral of depression is that it doesn't just get you down, it keeps you down. Depression is a very stable state—your brain tends to think and act in ways that keep you depressed. All the life changes that could help your depression just seem too difficult. Exercise would help, but you don't feel like exercising. Getting a good night's sleep would help, but you've got insomnia. Doing something fun with friends would help, but nothing seems fun, and you don't feel like bothering people. Your brain is stuck—depression pulls it downward, relentless as gravity. Your mood becomes like a marble sitting at the bottom of a bowl: whichever way you push it, it always rolls back down.

Depression is caused by the tuning of various brain circuits and their interactions with the world and with each other. Think of a simple circuit, like a microphone and a speaker. If they're oriented in a particular way, the smallest whisper can lead to screeching feedback. Orient them slightly differently and the problem is gone. But it's not a problem with the microphone. It's not a problem with the speaker. Both are working exactly as they're supposed to. It's a problem with the system and the interaction of the parts. The downward spiral of depression works in the same way and is shaped and directed by the specific tuning of your neural circuits.

We'll get a lot deeper into the specifics soon (with more scientific words, like "hippocampus" and "norepinephrine"), but depression generally involves a problem with how the *thinking* and *feeling* circuits in the brain get out of whack. While your brain can be divided into dozens of regions, the circuits that cause depression rely on relatively few.

Two parts of the brain in particular are to blame: the prefrontal cortex and the limbic system. To simplify, the prefrontal cortex is basically the *thinking* part of the brain, and the limbic system is the *feeling* part. In depression, something is off with the way these regions act and communicate with each other. The thinking prefrontal cortex is supposed to help regulate the feeling limbic system, but it's not doing a good job. Fortunately, it's possible to change the way they act and communicate, and that's what this book is all about.

What Is the Upward Spiral?

You can't always change where you are, but you can change where you're going. What if, instead of your life spiraling down, it spiraled up? What if you suddenly had more energy, slept better, hung out with your friends more, felt happier? Your neural circuits have just as much potential for this as they do for depression. It often takes only a few positive emotions to kick-start the process, which then begins to fuel positive changes in other areas of your life—this is the upward spiral, and its incredible efficacy has been proven time and again, in hundreds of scientific studies.[4] The question is, what's actually happening in the brain, and how does this spiral begin?

It turns out that positive life changes actually cause positive neural changes—in the brain's electrical activity, its chemical composition, even its ability to produce new neurons. These brain changes alter the tuning of your brain's circuitry and lead to further positive life changes. For example, exercise changes the electrical activity in your brain during sleep, which then reduces anxiety, improves mood, and gives you more energy to exercise. Similarly, expressing gratitude activates serotonin production, which improves your mood and allows you to overcome bad habits, giving you more to be grateful for. Any tiny change can be just the push your brain needs to start spiraling upward.

What's in This Book

This book is divided into two parts. The first explains why the brain gets stuck in the downward spiral of depression, detailing the circuits and chemicals involved. It will get pretty technical at times, but you don't need to be a brain surgeon to understand the basics of how your brain works. The first part focuses on understanding what you can change and accepting what you can't, which are both keys to an upward spiral.

The second part describes how specific life changes can change activity in various brain circuits to reverse the course of depression. Aside from understanding and acceptance, there are eight powerful life changes that contribute to the solution, and a chapter is devoted to each: exercise (chapter 5), decision making (chapter 6), sleep (chapter 7), habits (chapter 8), biofeedback (chapter 9), gratitude (chapter 10), social support (chapter 11), and professional help (chapter 12). In addition, there are helpful tips sprinkled through-out that you can take advantage of whether you have depression or not. For instance, if you need a scientific excuse to get a massage, see chapter 11.

The First Step

If you happen to be depressed and you're healthy enough to read this book, then you have what it takes to rewire your brain and reverse the course of depression. We've all got the same brain cir-cuits, so whether you're depressed or anxious or out of sorts or doing just fine, you can use the same neuroscience to improve your life. Your brain is a positive feedback system—often, all it takes to see effects is a tiny change, just as a butterfly flapping its wings in Los Angeles can break up a storm in New York. Even the act of reading this introduction is a message to your brain that you're on the path to getting better.

Of course, this book can't provide the one big solution to depres-sion, because there isn't one. But there are many dozens of small solutions that add to more than the sum of their parts. Taking advantage of any one of the numerous solutions will start to help. The first step is the most important, and you're already there.

Part 1

Stuck in a Downward Spiral

Chapter 1

A Brain Map of Depression

Halfway through my senior year in college, everything felt overwhelming. It began with anxiety about the future, which, for some unknown reason, started looking bleaker and bleaker. I remember that my body felt heavy and slow, that I didn't feel like talking. Trying to pick classes seemed too difficult. Even food didn't taste as good. And then my girlfriend dumped me, probably because I'd been a pathetic lump for the past couple months. After that, I started having more aches and pains and had trouble sleeping. The New England winter felt particularly long and dark.

I didn't realize at the time how depressed I was, and I also didn't realize all the ways I was inadvertently preventing my brain from sinking down deeper. I was playing a lot of sports, and that actually changes dopamine signaling in the brain, which helps make life more enjoyable. And going to class not only altered the habit circuit in my brain, but it also meant that I had to spend some time out in the sun on my way to and from classes, which boosted my serotonin and regulated electrical activity in my brain during sleep. I lived with three of my best friends, and talking to them every day changed how the emotional circuits in my brain interacted with the planning circuits. I was completely unaware of all these brain changes, and yet they still saved me from getting worse.

I understand that most people with depression go through a much deeper and darker place, but the same neuroscience still applies. There is nothing fundamentally different about the brains of people with depression and without it. In fact, there's no brain scan, MRI, or EEG that can diagnose depression—it's simply a by-product of the brain circuits we all have.

As a neuroscientist specializing in mood disorders, I've come to recognize that everyone has depressive tendencies to a varying degree. That's just how the brain is wired. Thankfully, most people have wellness tendencies that keep them from getting stuck in the downward spiral of depression. For those who don't, there's hope: the last decade has seen remarkable advances in our understanding of the brain circuits involved in depression and, more importantly, how they can change. This chapter is an overview of those circuits. It's a lot of information, but we'll be revisiting these same circuits throughout the course of the book, so it's good to get a handle on them now. Don't get too bogged down in the details; it's the bigger picture that matters.

What Is Depression?

There's good news and bad news. We'll start with the bad: we don't exactly know what depression is. Yes, we know the symptoms and many of the brain regions and neurochemicals involved, and we know many of the causes. But we don't understand depression in the same detailed way that we understand other brain disorders, like Parkinson's or Alzheimer's. For example, in Parkinson's disease, we can point to the death of certain dopamine neurons. In Alzheimer's, we can point to specific proteins. But the neural causes of depression are much more nuanced.

Do you have depression? If you have five or more of the following symptoms nearly every day for two weeks, then you may have Major Depressive Disorder (but only a mental health professional can make an accurate diagnosis). If you have fewer symptoms, you may have low-level depression. Either way, you can still benefit from the upward spiral.

- Depressed mood, such as feeling sad or empty or even constantly irritable

- Decreased interest or pleasure in all—or almost all—activities

- Significant (and unintentional) weight loss, weight gain, or decrease or increase in appetite

- Insomnia or increased desire to sleep

- Either restlessness or slowed behavior that can be observed by others

- Fatigue or loss of energy

- Feelings of worthlessness, or excessive or inappropriate guilt

- Trouble thinking, concentrating, or making decisions

- Recurrent thoughts of death or suicide[1]

Whereas most diseases are defined by their cause (for example, cancer, cirrhosis of the liver), the disorder of depression is currently defined by a collection of symptoms. You feel crappy most of the time. Nothing seems interesting, and everything seems overwhelming. You have trouble with sleep. You feel guilty and anxious and have thoughts that life isn't worth living. These are the signs that your brain circuits are caught in the downward spiral of depression. And if you've got enough symptoms, you're diagnosed with depression. There's no lab test, no MRI scan; it's just the symptoms.

The good news is that we know enough about depression to help you understand what's happening in your brain and how to get better. As you'll find out later in the book, exercise, sunlight, specific sleep patterns, certain muscle movements, and even gratitude all alter activity in specific neural circuits, reversing the course of depression. And in fact, it doesn't strictly matter if you have a diagnosable level of depression or not. Whether you have some anxiety or are just feeling out of sorts, the same neuroscience principles can give you a better understanding of your brain and how to make it work better.

Depression as a Traffic Jam

The flow of traffic through a city is complex and dynamic—sometimes jamming up inexplicably and other times flowing smoothly, even at rush hour. The stock market and larger economy follow similar patterns, as does the weather and even pop culture. Mathematically, these types of complex, dynamic systems share many similarities, including the way the whole system—whether a traffic jam, a tornado, a recession or a recovery, a viral tweet, or the next fad—can get caught in a runaway pattern: either an upward or downward spiral.

So why do tornadoes happen in Oklahoma but not in New York? Because the conditions are just right—the flatness of the land, temperature changes, humidity, and wind direction and speed. But there's nothing wrong with Oklahoma.

The same is true of your brain. In depression, there's nothing fundamentally wrong with the brain. It's simply that the particular tuning of the neural circuits creates the tendency toward a pattern of depression. It has to do with the way the brain deals with stress, planning, habits, decision making, and a dozen other things—the dynamic interaction of all those circuits. And once the pattern starts to form, it causes dozens of tiny changes throughout the brain that create a downward spiral.

The good news is that in complex systems like the brain, small changes can sometimes have big effects. Changing the timing of a single stoplight may cause or prevent a traffic jam. A YouTube video may go viral from a single tweet. And sometimes tweaking the tuning of one brain circuit can start to reverse the course of depression. Luckily, decades of scientific inquiry have shown us how to modify different brain circuits, change the levels of various neurochemicals, and even grow new brain cells.

Neuroscience 101

Before we get into the specific neuroscience of depression, let's talk about some brain basics. Your brain is composed of billions of *neurons*, tiny nerve cells. Neurons provide the computing power in the brain, like billions of tiny microchips. Neurons are constantly talking to each other by firing electrical pulses down their long branches, which function like electrical wires. When an electrical pulse reaches the end of a branch, the neuron squirts out a chemical signal, a *neurotransmitter*. Neurotransmitters transmit information by floating into the space between neurons—the *synapse*—and binding to the next neuron. So the whole brain is just billions of neurons sending electrical signals that turn into chemical signals in order to communicate.

Each electrical pulse—and resulting squirt of neurotransmitter—is not an order commanding the next neuron's actions; it is more like a vote on what the next neuron should do. The whole pattern of activity is like a presidential election. Everyone votes on who the president should be, and depending on those votes, the country veers off in one direction or another. If you can change the number of votes in a few key swing states by only a few percentage points, you can dramatically change the course of the country. The same is true of the brain. By changing the firing rate of neurons in a few key regions, you can influence the pattern of activity in the entire brain.

It might sound rather chaotic to have billions of interconnected neurons, but they're organized in very specific ways, clumped into smaller regions throughout the brain. Some regions are on the surface of the brain, the *cortex*. The term "surface" can be misleading, because the brain is so wrinkled that some cortical regions are actually pretty deep. But in contrast, there are even deeper regions, the *subcortical regions*, that are evolutionarily more ancient.

The neurons within each region talk to each other, as well as to other regions across the brain. These networks of communicating neurons are called *neural circuits*. Your brain works like a series of little computers all connected to each other.

As I said in the introduction, you've got dozens of different circuits that control every aspect of your life. Many of these circuits rely on the same overlapping brain regions, and all these various circuits influence each other. If you're feeling depressed or happy or hungry or horny, it's the result of the way a whole bunch of circuits are impacting each other.

The Chemicals of Depression

Picture the flight map in the back of an in-flight magazine showing all the cities an airline flies to and from. That'll give you a pretty good idea of the organization of a *neurotransmitter system*, which simply means all the neurons that release or react to a particular neurotransmitter. For example, the serotonin system is all the neurons that release or react to serotonin (just as the Delta "system" would be all the cities Delta connects to). Your brain relies on numerous neurotransmitter systems for different types of processing, and they contribute to depression in different ways.

In the 1960s, depression was thought to be a matter of having too little of the neurotransmitter norepinephrine. Then, a few years later, the theory changed to a deficiency of serotonin. We now know it's much more complicated. Sure serotonin and norepinephrine are involved, but so are dopamine and numerous other neurochemicals.

A whole bunch of neurotransmitter systems influence—and are influenced by—depression. This is a long list, but most of it will be revisited several times throughout the book. You don't need to remember it all now, just know that each neurotransmitter system has a few primary effects:

- Serotonin—improves willpower, motivation, and mood

- Norepinephrine—enhances thinking, focus, and dealing with stress

- Dopamine—increases enjoyment and is necessary for changing bad habits

- Oxytocin—promotes feelings of trust, love, and connection, and reduces anxiety

- GABA—increases feelings of relaxation and reduces anxiety

- Melatonin—enhances the quality of sleep

- Endorphins—provide pain relief and feelings of elation

- Endocannabinoids—improve your appetite and increase feelings of peacefulness and well-being

Go out in the sunlight. Bright sunlight helps boost the production of serotonin. It also improves the release of melatonin, which helps you get a better night's sleep (chapter 7). So if you're stuck inside, make an effort to go outside for at least a few minutes in the middle of the day. Go for a walk, listen to some music, or just soak in the sun.

This is an oversimplification, but in general, each neurotransmitter contributes to a different depressive symptom. A dysfunctional serotonin system is responsible for the lack of willpower and motivation. The difficulty in concentration and thinking is probably due to problems with norepinephrine. Dysfunction in the dopamine system leads to bad habits and lack of enjoyment. All of these neurotransmitters are necessary for proper functioning of dozens of circuits throughout the brain, and to make things more complicated, they all interact. Unfortunately, depression is not just a matter of not having enough norepinephrine, serotonin, and dopamine, and thus it's not solved by simply increasing the levels of these neurotransmitters. But that is *part* of the solution. Boosting serotonin leads to a better mood and a greater ability to set goals and avoid bad habits. Increasing norepinephrine means better concentration and lower stress. And more dopamine generally means more enjoyment.

This book describes how small life changes can change the activity of these neurotransmitter systems. The mechanics are quite complicated, but here's the gist. Essentially, the phrase "increasing serotonin activity" can mean a number of different things. It can mean that your brain makes more serotonin or increases receptors for it, or that those receptors just become stickier to serotonin. It can also mean that the serotonin that's made isn't broken down as quickly or that the serotonin squirted into the synapse just hangs out for a while—giving it a longer opportunity to bind to the next neuron—instead of being quickly sucked back into the neuron. Changing any one of these factors can increase serotonin activity. For example, most antidepressant medications work by blocking serotonin-sucking proteins (known as *serotonin transporters*), thereby increasing the amount of serotonin that can act on receptors.

In addition to neurotransmitters, other neurochemicals can also have dramatic effects. For example, *brain-derived neurotrophic factor* (BDNF) aids in the growth of new neurons and overall brain health. Even certain chemicals from the immune system can change neural signaling and show altered activity in depression.[2] But enough about the individual chemicals involved; let's get to the circuits.

The Basic Circuits of Depression

As I mentioned in the introduction, depression is primarily a result of poor communication between the thinking prefrontal cortex and the emotional limbic system. Together, these parts of the brain are often called the *fronto-limbic system*, because they form a group of closely interacting regions, the way Europe is a group of closely interacting countries. The fronto-limbic system regulates your emotional state, and when not functioning, it well can push you into depression.

Below we'll look at all the major players in the fronto-limbic system and the regions that communicate closely with them. I'm about to drop a whole list of names, but don't worry about remembering all the details now; we'll continue to revisit them throughout the book.

The "Thinking" Brain

The *prefrontal cortex* gets its name from the fact that it is the front-most part of your brain. Basically, it is the whole surface of the front third of your brain, sitting just behind your forehead. It is the CEO of the brain—the center of your planning and decision-making circuits. It is also responsible for controlling impulses and motivation.

The prefrontal cortex is the most recently evolved part of the cortex, and humans have more of it than any other animal. Our big prefrontal cortex gives us a huge evolutionary advantage, but it can also cause problems. In depression, it is responsible for worrying, guilt, shame, problems with thinking clearly, and indecisiveness. Changing activity in the prefrontal cortex can help with these problems, and it can change bad habits and improve willpower.

The prefrontal cortex can be arranged along two axes—vertical and horizontal—which basically divide it into four quadrants.

The Prefrontal Cortex

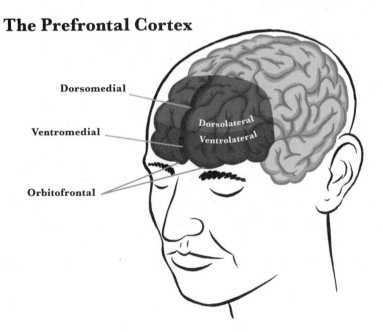

These quadrants are essentially the top-middle, top-side, bottom-middle and bottom-side areas of the prefrontal cortex. Of course, scientists like fancier words than that, so the parts near the top are called "dorsal" (like the dorsal fin on a dolphin), and parts toward the bottom are called "ventral" (from the Latin word for "belly"). Parts near the middle are "medial," while things near the sides are "lateral." For example, your nose is more medial than your eyes.

Each quadrant of the prefrontal cortex is primarily responsible for a different group of functions. The medial parts are more self-focused, while the lateral parts are more focused on the outside world. Along the vertical dimension, the ventral parts are more emotional, while the dorsal parts are focused more on thinking. Thus the primary distinction in the prefrontal cortex is between dorsolateral and ventromedial (in other words, the top-side versus the bottom-middle). The ventromedial prefrontal cortex is the more self-focused, emotional part of the prefrontal cortex and is particularly important in motivation and controlling your impulses. Calling it "emotional" might seem confusing, since I've said that the limbic system (rather than the prefrontal cortex) is the emotional part of the brain, but think of it this way: the ventromedial prefrontal cortex *thinks* about emotions, while the limbic system *feels* them. In contrast, the dorsolateral prefrontal cortex thinks more about the outside world and is thus more responsible for planning and problem solving.

Pretty much the whole prefrontal cortex is affected by depression.[3] Not feeling any motivation? It's likely the fault of reduced serotonin in the ventromedial prefrontal cortex. Finding it difficult to make plans or think clearly? It's probably disrupted activity in your dorsolateral prefrontal cortex. However, most problems, like difficulty in following through with plans, cannot always be pinpointed to one region or neurotransmitter system and often result from the communication between several of them.

The "Feeling" Brain

In contrast to the highly evolved prefrontal cortex, the limbic system is an ancient collection of structures located much deeper in the brain (even early mammals one hundred million years ago had limbic systems). The limbic system is the emotional part of the brain and is responsible for things like excitement, fear, anxiety, memory, and desire. It is primarily composed of four regions: the *hypothalamus*, the *amygdala*, the *hippocampus*, and the *cingulate cortex*. The hypothalamus controls stress. The amygdala is the key to reducing anxiety, fear, and other negative emotions. The hippocampus is responsible for creating long-term memories, and because its neurons are very sensitive to stress, it often acts as the canary in the coal mine of depression. Lastly, the *cingulate cortex* controls focus and attention, which is of huge importance in depression, because what you focus on, whether by automatic habit or willful choice, makes a huge difference to your mood.

The Limbic System

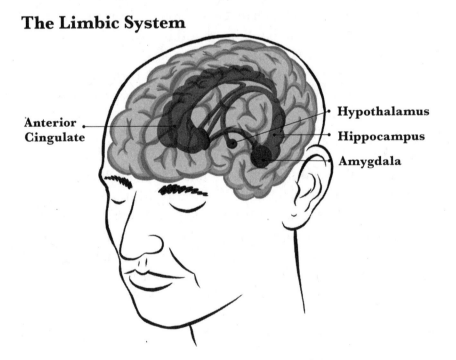

Anterior Cingulate

Hypothalamus

Hippocampus

Amygdala

Stress and the Hypothalamus

Feeling tense? On edge? Elevated stress is both a cause and a symptom of depression, and it can be attributed to the hypothalamus in the central limbic region. The hypothalamus regulates numerous hormones and controls the body's stress response. It can send your body into fight-or-flight mode, raising stress hormones like cortisol and adrenaline. It's like a military base waiting to deploy troops to deal with threats. When you're depressed, it's a base on high alert—it has a hair-trigger response, making it difficult to relax and just be happy. Finding ways to calm the hypothalamus is therefore one of the best ways to reduce stress.

Anxiety and the Amygdala

As a kid, I never would have said I had anxiety; I just got lots of stomachaches when I had to take tests or while waiting in line for scary roller coasters. But lo and behold, as I grew into a calmer adult, my stomachaches went away.

Anxiety isn't always obvious, but increased anxiety, in one form or another, is a symptom of depression. Anxiety is primarily mediated by the amygdala, an ancient structure deep in the brain, which is closely connected to the hypothalamus and is a central part of the emotional limbic system. People with depression often have higher amygdala reactivity, so reducing that can help lower anxiety and relieve depression.[4]

Memory and the Hippocampus

When was the last time you were truly happy? People with depression often have trouble remembering happier times but have no problem recalling sad events. This memory bias can be blamed on the hippocampus, which sits deep in the brain, adjacent to the amygdala; it also has strong connections to the hypothalamus. The primary job of the hippocampus is turning short-term memories into long-term ones, like hitting "Save" on a new document to store it on your computer's hard drive. The hippocampus is the "save" button; without it, you couldn't form new memories. It particularly likes to save emotional memories (like building your first snowman, the embarrassing thing you said to your crush in middle school, that great ski trip you took last year). That's somewhat problematic in depression, because the new memories your hippocampus forms will skew to the negative.

However, the hippocampus does much more. It is also central to *context-dependent memory*, which is the fact that it's easier to remember things that relate closely to your current situation.[5] For example, it's easier to recall memories from your undergraduate days if you're visiting your old college campus, because the context is the same. Unfortunately, in depression, there is a large downside to context-dependent memory. Because the "context" is depression, all those happy memories that are easy to recall when you're in a good mood suddenly evaporate. Meanwhile, all the tragedies in your life become too easy to remember.

In depression, the hippocampus not only shows abnormal activity but also tends to be smaller in size.[6] The small hippocampus is likely the result of chronic stress, which can damage and kill neurons. Depression is stressful and thus disrupts the proper functioning of the hippocampus. Fortunately, it's possible to grow new neurons in the hippocampus, and we'll cover that later in the book.

Attention and the Cingulate Cortex

When I was feeling overwhelmed in my senior year of college, I had a hard time paying attention in class, and I couldn't shake the feeling that I kept messing everything up. Difficulty concentrating is another symptom of depression, as is a greater focus on the negative, both of which are mediated by the cingulate cortex. In particular, the front of the cingulate—the *anterior cingulate*—has the biggest impact on depression. The anterior cingulate is covered by the prefrontal cortex and is closely connected with it, often functioning as a gateway between limbic and prefrontal regions. The anterior cingulate notices all your mistakes, plays a central role in the pain circuit, and contributes to the tendency to dwell on everything that's going wrong.[7]

> **Think of happy memories.** Happy memories boost serotonin in the anterior cingulate (chapter 8). Try to think of one happy memory before you go to sleep—write it in a journal or just reflect on it.

The anterior cingulate is like the screen on your computer. There's lots of data on your computer's hard drive, but the screen shows only the part you are paying attention to, and that has a huge impact on what you end up doing. In depression, anterior cingulate activity helps explains why you so often focus on the negative.

Interestingly, the neurotransmitter serotonin is highly concentrated in the anterior cingulate. That's important for depression, because serotonin is the neurotransmitter system most commonly targeted by antidepressant medications. In fact, activity in anterior cingulate can predict who will get better on antidepressant medication and who won't (shout-out to my dissertation).[8] In addition, directly stimulating the anterior cingulate with electrodes can vastly improve depressive symptoms.[9] Fortunately, there are ways to change anterior cingulate activity other than drugs or electrodes, which we'll cover later in the book.

The Connected Parts

In addition to the prefrontal cortex and limbic system, two other regions play important roles in depression: the *striatum* and the *insula*. Both are closely connected to the fronto-limbic system, and in fact, scientists sometimes lump parts of them into the limbic system.

Habits, Enjoyment, Addiction, and the Striatum

Depression is often accompanied by bad habits such as impulsiveness, poor coping skills, addiction, and procrastination. That can also include feeling fatigued and unmotivated. These bad habits are primarily caused by disrupted activity in the *striatum*, which is an ancient subcortical region deep below the surface that we inherited from the dinosaurs. The striatum has two main parts that are particularly important in depression: the upper part, known simply as the *dorsal striatum*, and the lower part, called the *nucleus accumbens*. Both parts rely heavily on the neurotransmitter dopamine to function properly.

The dorsal striatum is the brain's habit circuit; it controls most of your good and bad habits. Because your habits are behaviors you

The Striatum

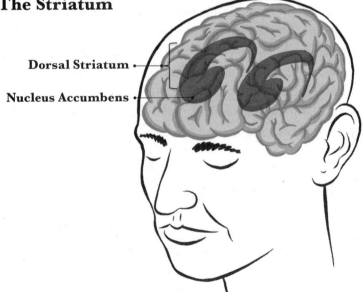

Dorsal Striatum

Nucleus Accumbens

do automatically, without thinking, once you create a good habit it has the power to change your life without conscious thought. In depression, reduced dopamine activity in the dorsal striatum is primarily responsible for feelings of fatigue.

In contrast, the nucleus accumbens is the "partier" of the brain. It is closely connected to the limbic system and is often considered part of it. It's largely responsible for impulsive behavior, like eating too many sweets or even drug addiction. Dopamine is released in the nucleus accumbens whenever you do anything fun and exciting—or at least it's supposed to. In depression, reduced dopamine activity in the nucleus accumbens explains why nothing seems enjoyable.

Pain and the Insula

A woman gets in a minor car accident and ends up with whiplash. At first, her neck pain isn't too bad, and her doctor tells her it will get better in a few weeks. But then it starts getting worse. She tries not to turn her head for fear of causing shooting pain. Her

The Insula

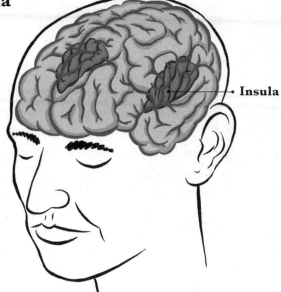

Insula

doctor's stumped, because her MRI suggests that everything should be normal. But the pain grows so bad that it becomes tough for her to drive, go to work, or even leave the house. She slowly grows more isolated and depressed.

Not everyone develops chronic pain from injuries, but unfortunately, some people have brains that are more reactive to pain, and this puts them at risk for a downward spiral. People with depression are more likely to suffer from chronic pain and tend to worry more about getting sick. These symptoms arise from an increased awareness of bodily sensations, which is mediated by the *insula*.

The insula is part of the cortex that folds inward a couple inches from your ears, sitting close to the amygdala and hippocampus. It's one of the main regions in the pain circuit and contributes more generally to bodily awareness. In people with depression, the insula shows elevated activity,[10] because it is more highly tuned to notice pain, elevated heart rate, breathing troubles, and other bodily problems. Increased insula activity makes you hyperaware of any problems in your body, even if they're small, which is how molehills turn into mountains. Calming insula activity can therefore help reduce both pain and worries about getting sick.

It's All Connected

Each region described above has specific connections with other regions. Unfortunately, there are almost too many connections to keep track of, so I'll focus mostly on the regions themselves. But, just as an example, the anterior cingulate connects to the ventromedial and dorsolateral prefrontal cortex, the insula, and the amygdala. The dorsolateral prefrontal cortex connects to the ventral prefrontal cortex, as well as to the dorsal striatum and hippocampus. Parts of the ventral prefrontal cortex connect to the amygdala and nucleus accumbens. And the thigh bone's connected to the hip bone.

One brain region can be a part of several circuits. Think of each brain region like an airport, and each circuit as a different airline flying off to different parts of the country. Just as airlines operate independently, but rely on the same airports, independent neural circuits rely on the same brain regions. And because neural circuits rely on some of the same brain regions, they interact dynamically. With air travel, backups in Chicago can lead to delays in Denver or cancellations in Kansas City; similarly, in the brain increased emotional amygdala activity can change what the anterior cingulate focuses on, as well as the habits controlled by the dorsal striatum. And the neuroscience gets even more nuanced than that.

Different regions often rely on different neurotransmitters. For example, the prefrontal cortex relies a lot on serotonin and norepinephrine to function properly, whereas the striatum depends mostly on dopamine. This means that changes in these neurotransmitters can have big effects on these regions.

What's Wrong with My Brain?

That's a trick question. There's nothing wrong with your brain, just like there's nothing wrong with the air in Oklahoma—despite the devastating tornados. Similarly, the specific tuning of your decision-making circuit can contribute to your brain getting stuck in depression—as can the specific tuning of your habit circuit, your stress circuit, your social circuit, your memory circuit, and on and on—they can all potentially contribute to a downward spiral of depression, when the conditions are right.

It's important to understand that if you have depression, your brain's not damaged goods—we all have the same neural circuits, the same basic brain structure. However, the specific connections between neurons are different in every person, so the dynamic activity and communication that flow through your circuits is as unique as you are. The specific tuning of each of your neural circuits creates a tendency to resonate in a certain pattern. The whole system resonates with your thoughts, your interactions, and the events that happen to you, and unfortunately, each perturbation has the potential to set off the depressive pattern in your brain.

Each circuit has a certain standard pattern of activity and reactivity, and it varies among people. When a circuit is activated more easily, we say it is more *reactive* or *excitable*. For example, depending on the excitability of the worrying circuit, some people worry more, and some worry less. And depending on the neural connections in the decision-making circuit, some people are more decisive than others.

In my case, I have a tendency to feel lonely, particularly when I've been writing all day. I don't know why, but that's just the tendency of my social circuitry. Other writers might not feel the same, but that doesn't help me. So if I know that I have a tendency to feel lonely, I should just make a plan ahead of time to hang out with friends after a long day of writing. But there's the problem. Making plans often stresses me out. I don't know why, but that's just the tendency of my planning circuitry. Many people may enjoy making plans, but not me. For me, the tendencies of these two brain circuits could get me caught in a downward spiral. The loneliness makes me feel bad and could be solved by making plans, but making plans stresses me out and also makes me feel bad. And the worse I feel, the harder it is to make plans. So these two circuits feed off each other and snowball out of control, like the interaction between the microphone and speaker that creates screeching feedback.

Given that I know my tendencies, I can choose to write at a coffee shop instead of staying at home; or I can meet a friend for lunch afterward, go for a run, or make any one of a dozen tiny life changes that could improve my situation. And in fact, once I realized this, I found my mental health greatly improved.

My friend Janice doesn't have a problem with loneliness or decision making—she has a different one. She needs to exercise every day, otherwise her mood plummets. That's just how she's wired. The problem is that when she feels down, she doesn't feel like exercising. So she doesn't and then feels even worse. Her brain has set her up for a downward spiral.

Sometimes the best solution is not always the most straightforward one. It turns out that other activities—like hanging out with friends, getting a better night's sleep, or even expressing more gratitude—could all help Janice's brain jump out of its rut. Because all of our brain circuits interact to keep us stuck, changing activity in one circuit can have a ripple effect across the whole system.

People have different things they worry about and different triggers that stress them out. For some planning is stressful, but for others planning can be comforting. Some people worry a lot about being alone, and others need lots of alone time. The different tendencies of your various brain circuits mean that everyone has different downward spirals they're likely to get stuck in and thus different upward spirals that will make them feel better. The trick is finding the right one for you, and hopefully this book will help with that.

How Did Your Brain Get This Way?

My grandmother had depression so severe she had to be hospitalized, and my brain inherited some similar tendencies. In addition to genetics, there are many factors that tune your brain's circuitry. Your early childhood experiences, current life stress, and level of social support can influence your circuitry toward or away from depression.

Your genes aren't your destiny. They do, however, guide the development of your brain circuits. For example, a particular gene in the serotonin system affects the development of the anterior cingulate and its interactions with the amygdala, and it increases your risk for depression.[11] So your genes can give you brain circuitry that is more likely to get depressed.

Early childhood experiences also shape the tuning of your circuits, even including the stress your mother experienced while pregnant with you,[12] and your brain is still actively developing until you're at least twenty. And given that the prefrontal cortex takes the longest to mature, it's susceptible to stress for a long time. Stressful life events throughout childhood and adolescence can alter the development of neural circuits and change the levels of various neurotransmitters.

The third big factor that shapes the tuning of your circuits is the current stress level in your life. Are you working in a job you hate? Or are you unemployed? Is your mortgage looming over your head? Do you have health problems? Did your boyfriend just cheat on you? All of these elements engage the stress circuit in the brain, which can drag other circuits into a downward spiral.

The fourth factor is the amount of social support in your life. Humans are social animals. We need each other, and we're meant to be around other people. Time and again, scientific studies have shown that close relationships help protect against depression. Note that it's not the number of friends you have that matters, but the quality of those relationships. If you have no one to talk to or do things with, or if you feel disconnected from those around you, there's a large potential for a downward spiral.

Lastly, random luck also plays a role. That might be hard to hear, but it's true. Complex systems, like your brain, are influenced by tiny fluctuations. This explains why on some days there's a traffic jam, and on other days the cars flow smoothly. It explains why some YouTube videos go viral, and others remain in obscurity. And it explains why you feel great on some days and crappy on others. There is not always an explanation for every little variation in your mood, so don't drive yourself crazy looking for one.

The overarching reason your brain circuits act the way they do is evolution. The human brain has been evolving for millions of years, and variation among people is the raw material of evolution.

There might be things you hate about how your brain acts, but that's just a result of evolution—and there's usually a good reason for it. For example, sometimes it's good to be a little anxious; it means you're less likely to do something stupid. Sometimes it's good to feel guilty; it makes you less likely to hurt others in the future.

Using the Upward Spiral

Now you know that depression comes from problems with frontal-limbic communication, and that it happens because of the specific tuning of your neural circuits. What if you could change the tuning of one circuit just a tiny bit?

It turns out that just a little change can be enough to push you away from depression and up toward a happier state. That's because in complex systems like the brain, even a little shift can change the resonance of the whole system. You might have a forecast for rain, but then the wind changes direction, the humidity drops by just 1 percent, and the day is sunny instead.

So we may not understand depression completely, but we do know the circuits that contribute to it. In the next chapter, we'll dive further into the mechanics of these circuits and how the brain spirals downward. Then, in the second half of the book, we'll explore how you can reverse the course of that spiral and propel yourself upward.

Chapter 2

Trapped with Anxiety and Worry

The other day I invited some new friends over for dinner at seven. I was excited to impress them and planned to make butter-lemon tilapia. A little butter, a little lemon, and ten minutes in the oven. Boom! Right?

At six I started using my prefrontal cortex to plan all the steps. The rice would take about twenty minutes, plus time to cool. The oven needed to be preheated. The vegetables wouldn't take long to cook, but I needed to chop them first, so I decided to start with that. It all seemed pretty easy.

I got out the cutting board and was about to start chopping when I realized my apartment was a mess. There were newspapers scattered on the couch, clothes on the floor, and dirty dishes on the coffee table. My friends had never seen my place, and I didn't want them to think I was a slob. I had to clean up. No big deal, right? I started through the same type of planning as with dinner. But five seconds into that, I realized I also had to take a shower and get ready.

Crap. I could get the cooking started, but what if I didn't have time to take a shower or clean before people got there? I could clean first, but what if the food wasn't ready? And what if my friends were late? The food might get cold. I kept starting to do one thing, then changing my mind and starting another. And the clock kept ticking, so every minute I didn't start doing things as efficiently as possible was another minute lost.

Ultimately, I wasted twenty minutes worrying about how to get everything done on time, and I had to go through an entire emotional roller coaster to get there. In the end, I managed to finish everything only fifteen minutes late, which meant I would have done everything perfectly but for the worrying. And in my distraction, I had missed my friends' text message explaining they'd be half an hour late.

Yes, that's a silly example of how worrying can get in the way of living your life, but then again, almost all our worries look ridiculous to a third party. It's hard to explain exactly why you worry about some things, but you do, and it gets in the way of your well-being.

Sure, there are larger examples in my life, but they generally follow the same pattern. For example, when finishing grad school, I knew I needed to look for a job, but nothing seemed interesting, and I didn't want to get stuck in a job that wasn't interesting. I could go work for a big company, but was that selling out? And would I really find it meaningful? I could work for a start-up, but then what if that was too time consuming, and I didn't have time for fun? And what if it failed? Maybe I could teach, but would I make enough money to support a family someday? And where would I find a good teaching job? Maybe I could do something else entirely, but everyone would think I was stupid for wasting all this time on a PhD.

I was seeing everything that could go wrong. When I tried to think about my future, my heartbeat quickened, and I just felt overwhelmed. It was easier to not think about it, to ignore the fact that graduation was drifting closer and closer, which obviously only made things worse.

Whether a dinner party or my entire future, in each case, I was anticipating everything that could go wrong, and that made me think of more things that could go wrong, until I got stuck in a loop of worry, anxiety, and indecisiveness. It's uncomfortable to feel the weight of the future pushing down on you, to be caught in the brief moment between the mistakes you made in the past and the mistakes you're about to make in the future. Perhaps you understand the feeling.

Worrying and anxiety are two big symptoms of—and causes of—depression. Worrying is mediated mainly by connections between several parts of the prefrontal cortex and the anterior cingulate. By comparison, anxiety is mediated by circuits within the limbic system. So there's no reason to get upset with yourself for feeling anxious or worrying too much; it's just a by-product of your brain's evolution. Fortunately, understanding the brain circuits involved in worrying and anxiety can give you a better handle on the situation.

Why Your Brain Worries

It would be great if we never felt worried or anxious, but that's not the way our brains are wired. The circuits that helpfully allow us to plan, solve problems, and make decisions are the same circuits that lead to worrying. And the circuits that keep us out of danger are the same circuits that cause anxiety. It's like how the features that make a Ferrari so fun to drive (for example, a big engine) are the same features that give it terrible gas mileage. Not all good qualities are good for everything.

Make a decision. Anxiety and worrying are provoked by possibility, not certainty. In fact, many people are less happy when they have more choices, because they have more to worry about.[1] When everything is up in the air, the amygdala becomes more reactive.[2] So if you tend to worry, reduce your options and make quick decisions whenever possible. As soon as you make a decision, however small, everything starts to feel more manageable—we'll discuss this more in chapter 6.

One thing that makes humans special is the fact that we have so much prefrontal cortex. The prefrontal cortex allows us to solve complex math problems, assemble Ikea furniture, send astronauts to the moon, and throw successful dinner parties. Think of a chess game. How do you know which move to make? You look at the board and run through a mental simulation. You could move your knight, but then your opponent could take your bishop, although it would expose his or her king. So you should move your bishop first, then your opponent can't take it after you move your knight. All of those thoughts happen in the prefrontal cortex. It's like a virtual reality machine that allows you to imagine the future and predict the consequences of your actions. The dorsolateral prefrontal cortex is especially involved in this type of planning,[3] though the medial prefrontal cortex also connects with the emotional amygdala and is particularly important in deciding how you will feel about whatever future you're imagining.

So what's the difference between planning and worrying? The answer is really just the amount of emotional and self-oriented processing in the medial prefrontal cortex and anterior cingulate—how vigorously these regions react to potential future scenarios. Planning and problem solving both involve projecting yourself or other pieces of information into the future and evaluating how you would feel about a particular outcome. Worrying has that same feature but is colored with more negative emotions. Worrying worsens your mood, and when your mood is worse, you worry more, which is a classic downward spiral.[4]

In one functional MRI (fMRI—a type of brain scan that looks at blood flow) study, Italian scientists had participants think about areas of their life that worried them most. They looked at both people with anxiety and a control group. They found that both the controls and the anxious group activated the same prefrontal and limbic regions: the dorsomedial prefrontal cortex and the anterior cingulate.[5] That illustrates that people with anxiety disorders have the same neural circuitry for worrying as "healthy" people. The difference between the two groups was simply that the people with anxiety problems got stuck in their worrying. Essentially, the communication circuit between the prefrontal cortex and anterior cingulate got stuck in the "on" position.

When I was planning the steps to make dinner, I was engaging communication between the prefrontal cortex and the limbic system. My prefrontal cortex was running through possible simulations of the future and then interrogating the limbic system to see how I'd feel about it. The first time, when I was calm and just planning steps for making dinner, my prefrontal cortex had no problem sifting and organizing all the information. But then I had a brief thought—*What if I don't get everything done on time?*—and that led me from decisive planning to getting stuck in a worry loop and spiraling even further down toward anxiety.

We'll talk about anxiety in a second, but the basic idea is that when the limbic system is overactive, it's like turning up the volume of your negative emotions. At that point, simple planning becomes more difficult, because the normal frontal-limbic communication becomes overwhelmed by the limbic system's shouting.

When you're in a negative mood, almost all outcomes that your prefrontal cortex can calculate are tinged with a bit of negativity. Any choice you make feels like it's going to lead you down the wrong path, and you quickly become inundated with all of the bad things that could happen to you.

The Difference Between Worrying and Anxiety

In 1571, at the age of thirty-eight, Michel de Montaigne retired to his library tower and spent the next ten years writing essays. Reflecting upon his life, he noted, "My life has been full of terrible misfortunes, most of which never happened." Both worrying and anxiety are to blame for filling your life with imagined catastrophes.

Worrying and anxiety are distinct but related concepts—you can have worrying without anxiety and anxiety without worrying.[6] Worrying is mostly thought based, whereas anxiety has more to do with physical components like bodily sensations (such as an upset stomach) or associated actions (like avoiding a situation). Worrying involves the prefrontal cortex and its interactions with the limbic system, particularly the anterior cingulate, while anxiety involves only the limbic system, mostly interactions between the amygdala, hippocampus, and hypothalamus. In essence, worrying is *thinking* about a potential problem, and anxiety is *feeling* it.

Pay attention to what you can control. If the future were completely under our control—or at least predictable—there would be nothing to be anxious about. Feeling in control reduces anxiety, worrying, and even pain.[7] These effects are mediated by the dorsolateral prefrontal cortex, so strengthening dorsolateral activity helps create an upward spiral.[8] You can do this by simply paying more attention to what *is* in your control, which helps modulate your brain activity and quickly reduces anxiety.

Whatever their differences, worrying and anxiety can both get in the way of living a good life. When you're using your planning and problem-solving circuitry to worry, you can't use that part of your brain for more important things, like excelling at your job or organizing a dinner party. It keeps you from focusing on what you're doing and often makes it harder to connect with other people. Most importantly, it can be exhausting. Anxiety makes most situations feel more difficult than they need to be, which saps your joy.

Another problem with worrying and anxiety is that they often trigger each other. And I'll give you ten points if you already identified that as a downward spiral.

Why Your Brain Is Anxious

As we briefly discussed above, anxiety depends on activation of the fear circuit—the same neural circuitry that keeps us out of danger. Fear activates the body's stress response, readying you to either face the danger or run from it. This is mediated by the limbic system, mainly in connections between the amygdala and hypo-thalamus. The amygdala is responsible for recognizing dangerous situations, and the hypothalamus activates the fight-or-flight response (a.k.a. the sympathetic nervous system), triggering the release of stress hormones like cortisol and adrenaline.

> **Take a deep breath.** Taking a slow, deep breath—inhaling and then exhaling slowly—actually calms down the sympathetic nervous system and reduces stress (as discussed in more depth in chapter 9).

Anxiety and fear activate the same stress response in brain and body, but anxiety is different from fear. The difference is between *actual* danger and *potential* danger. Fear is a response to actual danger that is right here, right now, while anxiety is concern for events that only *might* happen—events that may be unpredictable and that you may lack control over. Put another way, fear comes from seeing a lion jump out of the grass and start running toward you. Anxiety comes from seeing the grass rustle and assuming that a lion is hiding there. And anxiety is connected to anticipation of danger, which is why some people avoid fields of grass altogether, because there might be a lion out there. Anxiety activates the limbic system in the same way that fear does—as when you actually see the lion jump out at you—and while this may seem unfortunate, the sensitivity of the limbic system is actually one of its greatest evolutionary advantages.

> **Go for good enough.** Worrying is often triggered by wanting to make the perfect choice or by trying to maximize everything. When buying a used car, you want one that is cheap, reliable, safe, sexy, the right color, and fuel efficient. Unfortunately, no single option is likely to be the best in all those dimensions. If you try to have the best of everything, you're likely to be paralyzed by indecision or dissatisfied with your choice. In fact, this kind of "maximizing" has been proven to increase depression.[9] So don't try to make the most amazing dinner; start out by just making a good dinner. Don't try to be the perfect parent; just be a good one. Don't try to be your happiest; just be happy.

While the prefrontal cortex evolved to figure out complex problems, the limbic system is more of a trend-spotter, idea-connector, and pattern-finder. Whenever something bad happens (like getting chased by a lion), the limbic system tries to figure out everything that led up to that event so that it can avoid it in the future. Your brain accomplishes this through communication between the amygdala and the hippocampus. Since the hippocampus is responsible for memory, when something bad happens, your limbic system tries to connect the bad thing to something in your recent memory that might have predicted it. That way, in the future, it can predict the bad thing before it happens.

Imagine you're a baseball pitcher and you have a hat you always wear, and then one day you don't wear that hat, and you lose the game and feel ashamed. Your limbic system wants to avoid that feeling in the future, so it notices, "Hey, I forgot to wear my hat. That must be the reason I lost." Even though not wearing your lucky hat probably didn't cause the loss, once your limbic system assumes a possible connection, it becomes hard to unlearn it. From then on, not wearing the hat triggers anxiety. Anxiety doesn't always have a conscious, thinking component; it can simply be a sensation, like an upset stomach or shortness of breath. Often when you think you're sick, it's actually the physical manifestation of anxiety.

Why Worrying and Anxiety Can Be Good

There's nothing inherently better about people who worry less or feel less anxiety, nor is it always advantageous. Sometimes worry and anxiety can be useful. Your brain evolved that way to keep you alive. Worrying makes you think deeply about problems, rather than just taking the first answer that comes to mind, and anxiety helps keep you safe. If you always waited until you were in a dangerous situation before you activated the fear response, you'd be getting into a lot of dangerous situations. A million years ago, some early human looked at a cave and said, "I think I'll go check it out." His friend was a little more anxious and grunted back, "Not sure that's such a good idea." And guess what? The first guy got eaten by a bear and the second guy is your ancestor.

So don't get too upset with yourself for being anxious. Your brain is trying to help you. Unfortunately, the specific tendencies of your anxiety and worrying circuits sometimes interfere with your ability to be happy. The problem is only that these circuits might activate too frequently or might interact with each other to keep you stuck. Fortunately, recognizing how your brain works is a key step toward mindfulness and acceptance, which can help combat the worry and anxiety.

The ABCs of Anxiety

Jerry gets uneasy in airplanes, elevators, and tall buildings. Anya is uncomfortable talking to strangers and doesn't like going to parties. Dana gets heart palpations when she has to give a presentation at work. There are many different types of anxiety. There's social anxiety and performance anxiety and even general anxiety, which makes you anxious about everything. But they all follow the same basic pattern, and it's as easy to remember as ABC.[10]

"A" stands for "alarm." You make an observation that something seems wrong (for example, *My heart is racing* or *That tuft of grass seems to be shaking strangely*). Depending on the situation, the alarm is mediated by the anterior cingulate, the amygdala, or even the hippocampus. The anterior cingulate, which we'll talk about more in the next chapter, controls your attention and is designed to notice problems. The amygdala is also primed to detect threatening situations. Lastly, the hippocampus is particularly good at noticing subtle similarities between disparate situations. Any of these regions can trigger an alarm, and from there your brain moves to the next step in the pattern.

"B" stands for "belief." You evaluate the alarm and create a belief about the observation you just made (*I'm having a heart attack* or *There's a lion in the grass*). The beliefs are often subconscious; you're not even aware of them. The limbic system deals with unconscious beliefs, while the ventromedial prefrontal cortex deals with conscious ones.[11] In order to guide your behavior, you don't need a conscious thought like, *Oh, that field is dangerous*; a racing heart and squirming stomach are enough. What happens next determines whether it will all devolve into a downward spiral or not.

Avoid catastrophizing. Anxiety is exacerbated by envisioning the worst possible scenario—a process known as "catastrophizing" (for example, your friend doesn't call back immediately, so you conclude he or she doesn't like you anymore). It usually starts with a perfectly reasonable worry, and then, through an incorrect assumption, it snowballs out of control. Well, you can't control noticing the "alarm" in the first place, but you can reduce its negative impact. First, remind yourself of the more likely (and better) outcomes ("Maybe my friend is busy right now"). Second, whether or not the worst-case scenario is actually likely, make a plan to deal with it (for example, "If my friend doesn't call me back in three days, I'll just call again," or even "If my friend doesn't like me anymore, then I'll hang out with another friend"). Planning your response to stressful situations can increase prefrontal norepinephrine, and calm the limbic system, helping you feel more in control.[12]

"C" stands for "coping." Coping is whatever you do after the belief. Do you take a deep breath and tell yourself everything will be okay? Do you freak out? Yes, freaking out is a form of coping. But, while it gives you some semblance of control, it's not the most effective response. Nor is eating ice cream and watching television. Exercise is a more productive form of coping, as are calling a friend or breathing calmly; but if all these productive forms of coping were already part of your habit circuit, you probably wouldn't have a problem with anxiety. Coping is generally the realm of the striatum, which controls habits, and we'll cover that in chapter 4. And if you're trying to change your habits, then the prefrontal cortex gets involved, and we'll cover that in chapter 8.

Creating an Upward Spiral to Combat Anxiety or Worry

A coworker once confided in me how much "benzos" helped her anxiety. Benzos (a.k.a. benzodiazepines) are a medication that enhances the inhibitory neurotransmitter GABA and suppresses amygdala activity. But, there are also many ways to calm the anxious limbic system that don't require a prescription. In fact, your own prefrontal cortex is perfectly capable of soothing the amygdala and creating an upward spiral.

The first step is simply to recognize your anxiety or worrying when it occurs. Becoming aware of your emotional state activates the prefrontal cortex and allows it to suppress the amygdala. For example, in one fMRI study, appropriately titled "Putting Feelings into Words," participants viewed pictures of people with emotional facial expressions. Predictably, each participant's amygdala activated to the emotions in the picture. But when they were asked to name the emotion, the ventrolateral prefrontal cortex activated and reduced the emotional amygdala reactivity.[13] In other words, consciously recognizing the emotions reduced their impact.

One insidious feature of anxiety is that you might have a problem and not even realize it. Many people just notice physical symptoms and don't recognize that it's anxiety. If you have shortness of breath, dizziness, muscle tension, an upset stomach, chest pain, or just a general feeling of dread, it might be anxiety. Becoming conscious of it is a key step toward relieving it, because you can't fix something you don't know is there.

Amusingly enough, one of the most common ways people cope with anxiety is by worrying about it. In fact, worrying can help calm the limbic system by increasing medial prefrontal activity and decreasing activity in the amygdala.[14] That might seem counterintuitive, but it just goes to show that if you're feeling anxiety, doing something about it—even worrying—is better than doing nothing.

But as you might guess, worrying is not the most adaptive coping mechanism. It gives you a sense of control over a situation, however illusory, but unfortunately it does not free you from a downward spiral, just as ice cream (or whiskey) might make you feel better momentarily, but doesn't actually deal with the problem.

Furthermore, we often have anxiety about one thing, but worry about something else. For example, when I was worrying about getting the tilapia ready on time, that wasn't the real source of my anxiety. My anxiety centered on the awareness that my dinner might be late and my place was a mess—that was the "alarm"—and the resulting belief that my new friends might think I was an inconsiderate slob and wouldn't want to be friends with me. Worrying was just a misguided means of coping, and with all that riding on a piece of tilapia, no wonder I was a nervous wreck.

> **Stay in the now.** Pay attention to the things that are happening now, and don't pay attention to the things that aren't happening now. Focusing on the present helps reduce anxiety and worry, because it decreases emotional, self-focused processing in the ventromedial prefrontal cortex. Attention to the present also increases dorsolateral and ventrolateral prefrontal activity, allowing these regions to calm the amygdala.[15] Improving your ability to stay present, a practice known as "mindfulness," helps enhance these activations and leads to long-term improvements in anxiety and worrying.[16]

While worrying can be a temporary Band-Aid, the best way to calm the limbic system is to understand the underlying anxiety.

This is often a primary goal of psychotherapy, which we'll cover in chapter 12. For now, think of it this way: if you're planning a birthday party for your kid and are obsessively worrying over what kind of paper to use for the invitations, I can almost guarantee the real problem is not the paper. Maybe it's your spouse not being supportive or your mother being too critical. Only you can figure it out, and you can do this by examining your feelings. This self-examination activates prefrontal circuits, which can calm the limbic system. Putting emotions into words—however hokey that sounds—actually rewires your brain circuits and makes you feel better.

Another great solution is to focus on the present moment. Because worrying and anxiety are projections of yourself into the future, they're not things that exist when you are fully immersed in the now. So pay attention to what's going on right now. If there's an actual threat to your safety, then deal with it, but if it's just anxiety, simmering somewhere below the surface, then make a note of it—and move on. Shift your focus to what's occurring *right now*. This is why Buddhist monks and yogis practice *nonjudgmental awareness*—the process of being aware of the present, without attaching emotional reactivity to it. This mindfulness practice cuts off worry and anxiety at the source.

Since learning all of this, I've become more mindful. When I throw dinner parties now, I try to notice the beginning of a worry or anxiety spiral and not let myself get upset about it. It's just my brain working as it was designed. I acknowledge that the anxiety is rooted in something deeper than dinner and that figuring out what it is can help. But often I can cut it off by simply taking a deep breath, reminding myself that it will all turn out okay—or that if it doesn't, a ruined dinner party is hardly the end of the world—and then I go back to chopping broccoli.

Chapter 3

Always Noticing the Negative

I have ten minutes to get to a meeting, and I'm zipping past cars on the freeway. As I pass a big rig, I almost miss my exit and have to swerve across two lanes. A few pedestrians are jaywalking at the foot of the off-ramp, and I get annoyed that I might have to stop, but they cross before I get there. Three blocks later, I'm almost home free, just one more left turn. Maybe I can make it in time! And then, half a block away, I see the green light turn yellow and then slowly bleed red. Damn it!... Damn it, damn it, and a whole bunch of more interesting words.

Why does it seem like when you're running late, you always hit the longest red light in the world? And, of course, there would be a big rig and pedestrians getting in the way. But the real question is, why is my brain focused on the big rig that made me almost miss my exit and not on the fact that there was hardly any other traffic? Why did I get annoyed at the pedestrians even though they didn't actually get in the way? Why did I notice the red light and not the three green lights I had just driven through?

Sometimes it seems like the whole world is conspiring against you, like life is full of disappointing events, missed opportunities, and harsh circumstances. Maybe, for you, it feels that way all the time. But guess what? It's not some cosmic conspiracy, just a by-product of your brain circuitry.

You have a circuit in your brain that helps decide what to pay attention to and what to ignore. This attention circuit is influenced by the emotion circuit, so our brains are wired to pay more attention to emotional events. You have some conscious control over this, but most of it is automatic and unconscious.

Interestingly, our emotion circuits are more easily activated by the negative, which means that most people need to experience numerous positive events for every one negative just to come out even. Furthermore, some people's brains automatically focus more on the negative, which puts them at a greater risk for depression. Their brains are biased toward pain, loss, and the emotional toll of mistakes, and they often distort memories of the past and expectations of the future. In depression, the brain's negative bias is responsible for making bad situations seem a lot worse than they actually are. In truth, the reality is almost certainly better than it appears: your relationships not as broken, your job not as pointless, and your abilities greater than you realize.

The Emotional Brain Bias

A wooden chair, a ballpoint pen, an apple. If you saw pictures of these items, your brain wouldn't have a very strong response. But see a picture of a gun pointed straight at you—even though it's only a picture—and your amygdala suddenly goes into hyperdrive. That's because there's emotion tied to that picture, and everyone's brain is wired to pay more attention to emotional information than to just plain facts.[1] It turns out that the circuit for paying attention influences the circuit for emotion, and vice versa.[2] And while this is true of every human's brain, it is more exaggerated in people with depression, even in people at risk for depression.

Two brain regions in particular, the amygdala and the anterior cingulate, affect the interaction of emotion and attention. Importantly, both regions communicate closely with the prefrontal cortex and with each other. So affecting activity in one region can change the whole circuit and influence your emotional perception of the world.

Another example of your brain's automatic response to emotional information comes from a study in Switzerland. The researchers played recordings of angry or calm voices for subjects to hear.[3] But, interestingly, they played the voices at the same time: one in the left ear and one in the right ear. They asked subjects to pay attention to only their left ear or only their right ear. The researchers found that the amygdala responded to the angry voice whether or not the person was paying attention to it. The amygdala's response to emotion is not under conscious control. Other brain areas, however, like the orbitofrontal cortex, responded to the angry voice only when the person was consciously paying attention to it. This demonstrates that you do not have full control over your brain's automatic emotional response, but you do have some control.

In contrast to the general emotionality of the amygdala, the anterior cingulate has more defined roles in noticing the negative. Notably, the dorsal and ventral parts of the anterior cingulate play different roles. The dorsal anterior cingulate pays particular attention to pain,[4] to mistakes you make,[5] or to times when it thinks something might go wrong.[6] In short, it provides reasons for the amygdala to freak out. In contrast, the ventral anterior cingulate mediates feelings of optimism and helps rein in the amygdala.

The brain's inherent emotionality is exaggerated in depression. For example, one study showed that people with greater depressive symptoms, as well as those at risk for depression, were more likely to interpret neutral facial expressions as being emotional.[7] On top of that, they were more likely to misinterpret neutral expressions as being sad. Even when pictures contained no emotion, their brains added it. Think about the real-life consequences of this. Depressed people are more likely to believe friends are frowning at them, mocking them, or ignoring them—*even when they aren't*. It's easy to see how the downward spiral starts from there.

In addition, people with depression have brains that fixate longer on emotional information.[8] For example, in one study, people with and without depression were shown lists of emotional words during an fMRI scan. In people without depression, the amygdala activated for less than ten seconds, but for those with depression, it stayed active for more than twenty-five seconds. It's certainly difficult to be calm and rational when the amygdala hangs on to emotion for so long.

Now let's be clear—there's nothing inherently wrong with having a more emotional brain. After all, emotion adds spice and excitement to life. However, when increased emotionality is combined with increased perception of or attention to negative events, that can often spell trouble.

The Positivity Ratio

Unfortunately, all of our brains—no matter who we are—react more strongly to negative events. Negative events simply seem to carry more weight than positive ones.[9] Losing five dollars makes you more upset than finding five dollars makes you happy. Having a friend tell you you're beautiful doesn't quite balance out the effect of another friend telling you you're ugly.

The asymmetric response to positive and negative events is rooted in the brain's processing of emotion. Negative events cause greater self-referential activity in the medial prefrontal cortex and also increased activity in the insula, which is responsible for noticing visceral sensations.[10] Lastly, they also engage more of an emotional response in the amygdala and hippocampus.[11] These changes in brain activity suggest that we experience negative events more personally and we feel them more deeply.

All of this means that to be happy in our daily lives, we need a high ratio of positive to negative. And it turns out, after considerable study, that ratio is three to one. We need three positive comments from a friend for every negative one, three wins at work for every loss.[12] Of course, not everyone is the same. That three-to-one ratio is just an average. Some people might need only a two-to-one ratio and be fine, but others—people who feel losses and disappointments more deeply—might need a higher ratio. On top of that, if your brain simply ignores the positive events that happen to you—as is often the case with depression—you might need an even higher ratio.

Some Brains Have a Negative Bias

When I found out that I had been offered a contract to write this book, I was ecstatic—for about three seconds. Then I started worrying about everything I had to do, how much time it would take, and suddenly all I could think was, *Oh God, what have I gotten myself into?*

I have a remarkable capacity to notice the negative when everything is going right, and it serves me well in my many roles as a coach, writer, and scientist. I can spot an error in a theory. I can see problems with a defensive strategy and figure out how to make it better. I can anticipate what could go wrong in a given situation, which helps me plan for the worst. And it's often a helpful trait. For example, you wouldn't want an optimistic structural engineer— "I'm pretty sure that bridge will hold up." You want one who checks every calculation for a mistake; you want an expert at anticipating what might go wrong. Unfortunately, when this focus on the negative gets expanded to everyday life, it can dramatically impede our happiness.

So why can't you just focus more on the positive? What's wrong with you? If you just paid attention to the positive, you'd be more optimistic, less anxious, and far happier. As you probably already know, there are hundreds of books out there that will spend three hundred pages telling you this. Unfortunately, this philosophy often means people with depression get blamed for their own suffering—why can't they just snap out of it? Of course focusing on the positive is one of the central tenets to creating happiness, but it's not the whole story.

While it's true that everyone's brain is wired to respond more to emotional information, the type of emotional information that your brain is tuned to—and how it responds—differs across people. Some people's amygdalas are more reactive to emotional information[13] and require more effort from the anterior cingulate to avoid negative reactions. Others have a much easier time processing the negative and moving on. Consciously focusing on the positive can help, but some brain regions may still focus on the negative. The question is, which type of brain do you have?

The Negative Bias Doesn't Fall Far from the Tree

Take a look at your family tree. Are there a lot of branches suffering from depression or anxiety? Mood disorders run in families. The children of depressed parents have a higher chance of developing depression for many reasons, including genetics, early childhood experiences, and learned behaviors.

One group of researchers examined the heritability of the negative bias by studying the adolescent daughters of mothers with and without depression. They found that the daughters of depressed mothers had a greater bias toward noticing negative facial expressions.[14] Noticing negative emotions wasn't anything these girls were doing consciously; their brains just processed emotional information differently. Unfortunately, paying more attention to the negative puts them at risk for a downward spiral.

Other studies have found more links between genetics and depression. For example, one version of the gene that encodes for the serotonin transporter molecule significantly increases your likelihood of developing depression.[15] People with this copy of the gene have brains that pay more attention to negative emotions and less attention to positive ones.[16]

Importantly, this gene also negatively impacts brain regions that help with depression. For example, activity in the ventral anterior cingulate increases feelings of optimism[17] and also increases the chances a depressed person will get better.[18] People with this gene, however, tend to have a smaller, and thus less effective, ventral anterior cingulate.[19] Furthermore, this gene also reduces the ventral anterior cingulate's ability to calm the amygdala, meaning that people with this gene have amygdalas that are more reactive to emotional information.[20] Unfortunately, we're not done yet—there's something else that can send your brain into a downward spiral of negativity...

Mood Congruent Attentional Bias

"Life is a train of moods like a string of beads; and as we pass through them they prove to be many colored lenses, which paint the world their own hue." The poet Ralph Waldo Emerson understood how moods can change perception—a process called the *mood congruent attentional bias*. It turns out that when your mood gets worse, so does your brain's negative bias. Feeling down means you're more likely to notice negative things about the world and about yourself. This includes *context-dependent memory*, mentioned in chapter 1, which, in certain contexts, makes you less likely to remember happy events and more likely to remember sad ones.

A large part of this bias comes from the fact that being in a bad mood increases amygdala reactivity. The bad mood doesn't even have to be terribly bad to elicit a mood bias. In one study, subjects played a game of hangman, but the words used in the game were negative (like "nightmare"). After simply looking at negative words, the amygdala subsequently became more emotionally reactive.[21] So it doesn't take a lot to bias your brain.

Of course, as described above, this bias is even worse in people with depression. They tend to pay more attention to negative events and emotions[22] and to notice more sadness in the world.[23] Having depression is like being tuned to the six o'clock news *all the time*. If that was all you watched, you'd start to think the whole world was full of nothing but political scandals, weather disasters, and horrific crimes. If you could only change the channel, you'd see everything else that's out there—but you can't.

Fortunately, the same mood bias that gets you stuck in the negative can also help accelerate an upward spiral. When you notice something positive or improve your mood just a tiny bit, your emotion and attention circuits like to keep things rolling. We'll discuss modifying these circuits a lot more in the second half of this book, but first we'll take a deeper look at the types of negativity your brain notices.

Noticing Mistakes

Ever feel like nothing you do ever comes out right? Well, that's completely understandable, given that the upper (dorsal) part of the anterior cingulate is specifically tuned to notice your mistakes.[24] To be fair, the dorsal anterior cingulate is not a sinister spouse who's always pointing out your flaws; it's actually trying to help you. Your brain likes to take shortcuts if it can, and most of the time, it's on autopilot. But when your brain notices that you've made a mistake, the anterior cingulate alerts the prefrontal cortex, "Hey, this is something we should pay attention to. Time to use a little more processing power."

Notice what you notice. You can't control the random bits of information that pop into your head. But you can start to notice your biases. When you get annoyed that you're stuck at a red light think, *Oh, that's interesting. I noticed this red light, but I didn't notice the last green light I made.*

In short, try practicing *nonjudgmental awareness*. Nonjudgmental awareness is a form of mindfulness that simply means noticing without reacting emotionally, even when things don't turn out as you expected. Awareness does not require emotion, because emotion and awareness are mediated by different brain regions. Noticing a mistake might automatically trigger the emotional amygdala, but becoming aware of your own reaction activates the prefrontal cortex, which calms the amygdala.[25]

The dorsal anterior cingulate is just trying to help you do a good job. One fMRI study looked at how the anterior cingulate could modulate prefrontal cortex activity after errors. The study showed that once the anterior cingulate noticed conflicting information, it increased the responsiveness of the dorsolateral prefrontal cortex.[26] It's like a helpful friend who lets you sleep through high school chemistry and taps you on the shoulder when the teacher is about to call on you.

What does your brain do when it's not doing anything? Trick question: it's always doing something. The anterior cingulate is on by default. It's always looking over your shoulder watching for mistakes. Don't get too upset at it when it keeps pointing out your mistakes. It's just doing its job.

Being Pessimistic

Remember those pictures people were asked to look at? Some were positive (like a picture of a kitten), some were negative (like a gun), and some were neutral (like a chair). Most of the time, the participants were told what kind of picture they were about to be shown, but sometimes the researchers made it uncertain.

When people with depression were told they were going to be shown negative pictures, they had more activation in the insula and the ventrolateral prefrontal cortex, indicating more visceral and emotional processing than nondepressed people would have.[27] Surprisingly, when they weren't told about the type of picture, their brains still reacted as if expecting a negative picture. In the face of uncertainty, their brains assumed the worst. On top of that, when they were uncertain, depressed people also had more worried dorsolateral prefrontal activity, as well as more self-focused emotional processing in the medial prefrontal cortex. This response to uncertainty can explain why people with depression are more likely to be pessimistic—the past was negative, so the future must be too.[28]

It's important to understand your brain's response to uncertainty, because it can dramatically affect how you feel. When starting a new relationship or changing jobs, your brain may automatically interpret the new situation as something bad. But it's not bad; it's just unknown. And for almost anything worth having (true love, a great job) you have to pass through some period of uncertainty. We have to constantly remind ourselves that our brains may be skewing the unknown toward the negative, so we don't miss out on the potentially awesome rewards on the other side.

The Painful Part of Pain

One of the most negative things you can notice is pain. Isn't it strange how sometimes your body aches all over, and at other times you don't notice it at all? That's because your perception of pain is greatly influenced by your mood and motivation.

Pain isn't like other bodily sensations. It has an emotional component. We don't just perceive pain objectively (*Oh, my hand seems to be stuck in the car door*); we have an automatic emotional response to it, (*$#%^# car door! That %#$%^ hurts!*) The emotional component is really what puts the pain in the pain sensation.

The important distinction here is between pain signaling and pain perception. Pain signaling is carried out by neurons throughout your body called *nociceptors*, which bring pain signals to your brain. But just because a part of the body signals that there is pain doesn't mean it gets perceived by the brain as painful. For that, the anterior cingulate has to get involved.[29]

One fMRI study[30] looked at brain activity in depressed people as they were anticipating pain and also when they were actually feeling it. The study found that when anticipating pain, people with depression had increased activation in the insula, amygdala, and dorsal anterior cingulate. Thus, compared to nondepressed people, they had a more visceral and emotional response to the possibility of pain and even considered it more likely to occur.

Lower amygdala reactivity with a hug. A hug, especially a long one, releases a neurotransmitter and hormone called *oxytocin*, which reduces the reactivity of the amygdala (chapter 11).

Similarly, during actual painful stimulation, people with depression had greater increases in amygdala activity than nondepressed people. Their brains had a more emotional response to the pain. And the more helpless they felt, the greater the brain's emotional response. Furthermore, they had decreased activation in the region of the brainstem that produces painkilling endorphins, so their brains did not try to suppress the pain as much. They also had decreased activity in the ventral anterior cingulate and prefrontal cortex, which meant that the pain had a greater impact on their optimism circuitry and lowered their ability to think rationally about the situation. Thus, if a depressed person and a nondepressed person both burn their hand on the stove, the depressed person is more affected by the pain. The brain's response to pain is one reason that people with chronic pain are more likely to develop depression, and vice versa.

Bad Memories

In depression, there is a brain bias toward bad memories. No, I'm not talking about the kind of bad memory that makes you forget what you were supposed to buy at the supermarket. I'm talking about remembering only the bad stuff and forgetting the good stuff, which is caused by miscommunication between the amygdala and hippocampus.

The mood bias that affects your perception of the present also affects your memory, both the remembering of old memories and the creation of new ones. When the amygdala gets stressed, it tells the hippocampus to store that memory—just another way the brain evolved to help protect you from danger.[31] Unfortunately, this isn't an advantage in all situations. When you're depressed—and thus perceiving more negative events—those negative events are more likely to stimulate the amygdala and be encoded into memory by the hippocampus. Thus, in depression, you're more likely to store more bad memories than good ones. On top of that, because of context-dependent memory, depression makes it harder to remember happy memories and easier to remember bad ones.

Lastly, you might think your happy memories are safe from the mood bias, but unfortunately, old memories aren't retrieved like an old email; they're reconstructed from bits and pieces every time you remember them. Your negative mood influences that reconstruction so that you add a bit more darkness and sadness to them. Recognizing that you're viewing your own past through the sunglasses of your current depression can help you realize that your life hasn't always been this bad.

The Sting of Losing

Some people have brains that react more deeply to losses and disappointments. In one study, researchers examined people with a family history of depression, who are thus at higher risk for depression, and looked at the brain's response to winning and losing at gambling. The study found that when the people at risk for depression lost money unexpectedly, they had greater activation in the orbitofrontal cortex, which means losing had a greater impact on their motivation circuit. And when these subjects won money unexpectedly, they had reduced activation of the hippocampus.[32] Since the hippocampus is essential for memory, this reduced activity means that they're less likely to remember winning. Thus both their memories and their future actions are slightly altered by their risk for depression, which creates the potential for a downward spiral.

The researchers then gave the participants antidepressant medication for four weeks. While the medication did not affect their levels of depression or anxiety (remember that they weren't actually depressed, just at risk), it did affect their brain activity. After the medication, the orbitofrontal cortex was no longer so reactive to losing, and the hippocampus activated more on wins. So just because your brain circuits have a natural inclination toward negativity doesn't mean they have to stay that way forever. Maybe medication is the answer, or one of many other ways to modify brain circuits, which we'll discuss in later chapters. The point is that improvement is possible.

Reversing the Negative Bias

There are several ways to counteract both the inherent negative brain bias and the mood bias. While we'll cover more ways to alter this type of brain activity in the second half of this book, here are a few things you can do.

The Neurochemistry of Positivity

Two neurotransmitter systems play a particularly important role in reversing the negative bias: serotonin and norepinephrine. Both are commonly targeted by antidepressant medication, and both have a huge effect on the communication between the anterior cingulate, amygdala, and prefrontal cortex.

> **How to increase norepinephrine.** Surprisingly simple things can help increase norepinephrine—and thus decrease the negative bias—such as exercise, a good night's sleep, and even getting a massage. We'll discuss these in more detail later in the book (chapters 5, 7, and 11, respectively).

One study looked at the effect of using medication to boost serotonin or norepinephrine. After a week, neither medication significantly increased overall happiness, but they both caused increased attention to positive events and decreased attention to negative ones.[33] While this study was conducted on healthy volunteers, it suggests how antidepressants help with depression. They don't necessarily directly improve mood, but instead bias the brain toward noticing positive events.

Serotonin and norepinephrine are also important in pain processing. The medications that help with depression are also helpful for chronic pain, and they reduce pain-related dorsal anterior cingulate activity.[34] Chronic pain can be an incessant downward spiral, so reducing pain's effect on the brain can certainly be a great start to an upward spiral.

Strengthen Optimism Circuits

To combat pessimism, you can strengthen the brain circuits responsible for optimism. The first step is to simply imagine the *possibility* of positive future events. You don't have to believe they *will* happen, just that they *could* happen. It's possible you could find true love tomorrow. It's possible that you could find a better job. It's possible that things won't turn out in the worst conceivable way. Recognizing that good things are possible activates the lower (ventral) anterior cingulate.[35] Importantly, the ventral anterior cingulate helps regulate the amygdala, so admitting the possibility of good things helps control the brain's negative bias.

The second step to strengthening optimism circuits is not just recognizing that good things *could* happen, but expecting that they *will* happen. Expecting positive events also activates the ventral anterior cingulate,[36] as well as prefrontal areas that also help control the amygdala.

Of course, all of this is easier said than done. While it's not always easy to ignore the negative and focus on the positive, strengthening your brain's ability to calm the amygdala will help. Part 2 contains several techniques for accomplishing this, such as a good night's sleep (chapter 7) and hanging out with friends (chapter 11). Luckily, we're almost to part 2.

Chapter 4

Caught in Bad Habits

My friend Billi is the most interesting person I know, but he's had a hard life. He grew up extremely poor in a small Michigan town, across from the city dump, and both his parents were physically and verbally abusive. Despite his turbulent childhood and various drug habits later in life, he went on to play football for the University of Michigan, become a successful television writer, and ultimately earn a PhD in neuroscience. He has had to endure racism and homophobia and depression. On top of that, when I met him he weighed seven hundred pounds. While he has done a lot of work over the years I've known him to get his weight down, the work is still in progress. He has graciously allowed me to share his story here.

Unfortunately, Billi's weight problems and mood problems are intertwined. When he's feeling down or stressed, food makes him feel better. Yet being extremely overweight contributes to his depression (do I need to repeat "downward spiral" again?). He's so large he can barely fit in his car. If he weighed less, he would have fewer medical problems and would also have an easier time moving around, finding work, and hanging out with friends. He knows this, and yet for years he kept eating and eating. And it's not that he's dumb; he's brilliant (he does have a PhD in neuroscience after all).

He finds himself eating even when he doesn't want to. And when he feels stressed, he just wants to eat. But eating isn't his only bad habit—he also watches too much television and is chronically late to meetings. If he knows these things are bad for him, why can't he stop? Why can't he stop eating? Why can't he exercise more? Maybe you feel the same way about your own bad habits.

It's easy to be judgmental, because the habits that contribute to his downward spiral are so easy to see from the outside. Unfortunately, most of us have bad habits that are just as obvious—just not to us. For example, I have terrible problems with procrastination, and I end up watching television instead of writing or exercising. Maybe you've got a habit of giving up when things get difficult, and it keeps you from accomplishing meaningful goals. Maybe you have anger issues or organization problems. Maybe you push people away when you start to feel close, or just spend too much time alone. Maybe you never met a cookie you didn't like, or a cigarette or a can of beer. And in addition to the bad habits you know about, you probably have several others that are negatively impacting your life that you aren't even aware of.

Habits are, by definition, hard to change. And some habits are so deeply ingrained that we don't believe they can be changed. Fortunately, the first step to accomplishing change is simple awareness, and the second step is believing it to be possible. Which it is. You might need therapy or medication, or you may simply need to perform some of the activities described in this book. But first and foremost, you need an understanding of how your brain creates and controls your habits.

Controlling Actions

To really understand habits, you need to understand how your brain dictates your actions in general. We tend to think that most of our actions are driven by conscious intention. In fact, most are impulses or routines—not induced by a particular thought, just an automatic response. In a word: habits. This is particularly true in depression. And unfortunately, the habits that lead people into depression are not likely to lead them out.

There's a clear, neuroscientific logic to how habits are created and maintained, and also to how they're changed. While intentional actions are mediated by the prefrontal cortex, habits are controlled by the *striatum*, an ancient processing center deep in the brain. (If your prefrontal cortex is modern, cloud-based computing, then your striatum is punch cards fed into an IBM mainframe.)

So if bad habits aren't helpful to us, why do we keep doing them? Because the striatum, unlike the prefrontal cortex, is not rational, at least not in the way you usually define "rational." It doesn't distinguish between good and bad habits at all. The striatum is perfectly happy carrying out bad habit after bad habit with no regard to the long-term consequences. Before you get too upset about that, you should know that the striatum isn't even conscious. You can't really blame yourself for something you did while sleepwalking, so you can't really get upset at your similarly unconscious habits.

Bad habits can generally be classified as either impulses or routines. Impulses are actions driven by a momentary desire, like clicking on a Facebook link. By contrast, routines are not driven by desire but are actions we take simply because we've done them so many times before. A routine bad habit could be something as benign as chewing with your mouth open or something as harmful as withdrawing from the world when you start to feel overwhelmed.

Impulses and routines are both controlled by the striatum, but routines rely on the upper part, the dorsal striatum, while impulses are initiated by the lower part, the nucleus accumbens. Both regions rely heavily on the neurotransmitter dopamine, an important fact we'll discuss later.

The actions you take are the result of a conversation between the prefrontal cortex, nucleus accumbens, and dorsal striatum. The prefrontal cortex chooses what to do based on what's good for us in the long term. The nucleus accumbens chooses what to do based on what's the most immediately pleasurable. And the dorsal striatum chooses what to do based on what we've done before. Like members of Congress, these regions sometimes support each other and sometimes disagree. The prefrontal cortex is the only part of the circuit that cares about your long-term well-being, but unfortunately, it often gets outvoted. To understand why, we'll take a deeper look at impulses and routines.

Motivating Impulses

Checking out at the supermarket, you're presented with an array of enticing candy bars and magazines. Do you stick to your shopping list or reach for a Snickers? The key to understanding impulses is that everything pleasurable releases dopamine in the nucleus accumbens. Sex releases dopamine. Winning money releases dopamine. Drugs release dopamine. Chocolate releases dopamine.

The really interesting thing about the nucleus accumbens, however, is that it learns what's pleasurable and how to anticipate getting it. For example, when you eat a Snickers for the first time, dopamine is released in the nucleus accumbens. The next time you pick up a Snickers, dopamine is released as soon as you open the wrapper. And the next time, dopamine is released simply when you see the Snickers from across the room. Pretty soon, dopamine is released as soon as you walk into the store, just from the anticipation of seeing it, opening it, and eating it.

With impulses, something you do or sense triggers the anticipation of a specific pleasurable outcome. The problem is that the dopamine that is released in anticipation of pleasure actually motivates the actions that lead to that pleasure. Each step along the way gives you a little boost of dopamine that propels you on to the next step.

Figure out your triggers. It is much easier to avoid temptation than to resist it. If you know what triggers a particular habit, sometimes you can get rid of that habit simply by removing that trigger from your life. For example, Billi realized he was watching too much television, and the trigger was seeing the television set itself. So he moved it out of his bedroom, and now he doesn't have a problem watching too much television. As another example, if you don't want to buy cookies, don't walk down the cookie aisle at the supermarket. Seeing all those delicious baked goods will release dopamine and push you toward buying them.

If you were a caveman, your impulses wouldn't be such a problem. Life would be pretty simple. If something tastes good, you eat as much as possible, and if something feels good, you do it as much as possible. Nowadays, though, there are too many easily obtainable pleasures, which hijack dopamine in the nucleus accumbens and create a tendency to act for immediate gratification.

It becomes even more problematic in depression, because there's less dopamine activity in the nucleus accumbens. First, that means things that used to be enjoyable no longer are. Second, with reduced dopamine activity, the only things that motivate the nucleus accumbens are things that release lots of dopamine, such as junk food, drugs, gambling, and porn. All these impulses mean your actions are guided only by what's most immediately pleasurable, which is not usually good for you in the long term. And while most impulses are easy to recognize, the most insidious bad habits are often routines.

Developing Routines

There's an ancient Hindu saying: "For the first thirty years of your life you make your habits. For the last thirty years of your life, your habits make you." Do you ever eat when you're not hungry or continue watching television even though nothing good is on? Routines often cause downward spirals because we act them out even though we don't derive any pleasure from them. On top of that, we're often unaware when we've initiated them. Lack of pleasure and consciousness may seem odd, but in fact, the dorsal striatum doesn't much care about either.

The dorsal striatum has many strong ties to the nucleus accumbens, and it also utilizes dopamine. However, the dopamine released in the dorsal striatum doesn't make you feel pleasure; it just compels you to act.

Habits are formed because every action activates a specific pattern in the dorsal striatum. Each time you follow the same path, it becomes more and more defined in your brain—in other words, the neurons in the dorsal striatum are wired together more strongly. In addition, each time you activate that brain pattern, it becomes easier to activate the next time. So pretty soon, it's nearly impossible to create a new path—all your brain wants to do is follow old tracks.

The important thing to understand about a pattern in the dorsal striatum is that once it's there, it's pretty much there for good. That's why you never forget how to ride a bike. This is one of the reasons that bad habits are so hard to change. You don't actually eliminate old habits—they just get weaker as you create newer, stronger ones. Furthermore, once habits are in the dorsal striatum, they no longer care about pleasure. Sure, they usually first get in there because your nucleus accumbens is motivating you to do something, but once a habit is really engrained, it no longer requires the nucleus accumbens to motivate it.

That's also how addictions work. Addictions start out as pleasurable impulses in the nucleus accumbens. But over time, the nucleus accumbens stops responding, and the addictions no longer feel pleasurable. But because they are engrained in the dorsal striatum, you feel compelled to have another drink or another cigarette anyway. Because of these changes in dopamine, addictions increase your risk of developing depression, and depression increases your risk of developing an addiction. Another downward spiral.

The dorsal striatum doesn't care about what you want. It just cares about following paths that you've already carved out. Understanding the paths your brain follows is a key step to change. Unfortunately, sometimes the problem lies not in bad habits, but in doing nothing at all.

Fatigue

The alarm goes off on your bedside table, startling you awake, but you're not sure if you have the energy to turn it off. Many people wake up sluggish, but in depression, that same feeling can last the whole day—your energy drains away, and everything feels difficult. Fatigue is a common symptom of depression and is due both to the prefrontal dysfunction that we already discussed—such as reduced serotonin, which makes planning and decision making sluggish—and reduced activity in the dorsal striatum.[1] Proper prefrontal functioning is required to create new actions, so when the prefrontal cortex is disrupted, it lets the striatum take over. Thus, any actions you take will probably be old routines or impulses. However, since dorsal striatum activity is also reduced, unless you're motivated by an impulse, you're less likely to do anything at all. That explains why on some days it's just so hard to get out of bed.

Habits Are Triggered by Stress

In the critically acclaimed HBO show *The Wire*, Detective Jimmy McNulty has problems with drinking, anger, and fidelity. But when he transfers from the erratic hours, uncertainty, and stress of the homicide division to the more predictable beat of street patrol, everything changes. He stops drinking, calms down, and stays faithful.

In chapter 2, we learned that coping is the third part in the ABCs of anxiety. But coping doesn't just happen when you're anxious—it's a habit that helps us deal with any form of stress. Stress causes dopamine release in the dorsal striatum,[2] which automatically activates your coping habits. For McNulty, the stress came from the uncertainty of the job, and his coping habits were, to put it mildly, not the most productive.

Everyone has coping habits; they are some of the deepest, most ingrained routines we have. They make us feel better, at least for the time being, by reducing amygdala activity and the body's stress response. Good coping habits can pull you out of an impending downward spiral, because the dorsal striatum takes over and sets your life back on course. But bad coping habits don't stabilize your mood in the long term, so acting them out just creates more stress later on, and down the rabbit hole you go.

Coping habits do a lot to explain Billi's situation. Why did he eat so much? As a kid, with the chaos in his house, eating became his coping mechanism for stress. Eating provided a distraction, an immediate pleasure, and it also reduced his body's stress response. In the beginning, it was just an impulse to eat, but eventually it became deeply ingrained as a routine. Once a routine, pleasure was no longer a part of it, nor was attention, but it still provided a sense of control in a crazy world. It became an addiction. When he was stressed, if he stopped paying attention to his actions for even a few seconds, he would find himself walking to the kitchen or driving to McDonald's or calling up Domino's. Your oldest habits are probably the ones that used to distract you from life's greatest stresses, but now that your life situation has changed, they're no longer helpful. And yet you still do them, because they're there.

Unfortunately, by the time Billi realized that his coping habits were not optimal, he was in a bit of a pickle. His weight caused him a lot of stress, and his stress caused him to eat a lot. This is the case with all addictions: if you don't act on your habit, you feel anxious, which makes you want to act on the habit even more. And if you do yield to the habit, it just causes more stress later on, which retriggers the habit. It's easy to see how we get stuck in a cycle—how it can feel impossible to break out of.

But it's not impossible. To get rid of a destructive coping habit, you can't just stop doing it, because then you're left with the stress. Instead, you have to replace it with another habit. Billi was able to do this in a pretty ingenious way; he channeled his addiction to food into carving elaborate food art—a rose from an apple, a swan from a cantaloupe. When he felt compelled to eat, he now had something less destructive to occupy his attention. He also took measures to reduce the stress that triggered his bad habits, mainly through exercise, writing, and mindfulness. The combination of these things has helped him lose two hundred pounds in the first few years I knew him, and he is still on his way down. It's obviously a much harder struggle than I have described in only a few sentences, but it's achievable with more constructive coping habits and reducing stress in the brain—which we'll delve into in the second half of this book.

Stress Exaggerates Habits

Our coping habits are not the only habits triggered by stress. In fact, stress biases the brain toward any of our old habits over new actions.[3] The dorsal striatum says, "Let's do it this way, because we've always done it this way." And the prefrontal cortex says, "But that won't help us get where we want to go." Meanwhile, the nucleus accumbens says, "Ooh, that cupcake looks delicious."

Stress changes the dynamics of the conversation. When you're calm and relaxed, your prefrontal cortex is pretty good at getting its way. But the more anxious or stressed you get, the more the power shifts to the dorsal striatum and nucleus accumbens. That's why you might be doing fine on your diet until you get in a fight with your significant other. Or you might be exercising regularly until family drama raises its ugly head. When stressed, you usually act out your most deeply engrained routines or become a victim to your impulses.

> **Take a deep breath.** When you start to feel antsy or compelled to act on a bad habit, take a deep breath. Let it out slowly, then take another deep breath. Repeat as necessary. As we'll discuss more in chapter 9, long, slow breathing calms the brain's stress response.

Routines and impulses get worse when you're depressed, but they can get in the way of happiness whether you have depression or not. We'll learn about more of them later in this book: working habits (chapter 6), sleeping habits (chapter 7), eating habits (chapter 8), social habits (chapter 11), and more.

Controlling Impulses and Routines

Whether we're talking about impulses or routines, all bad habits are triggered by something. If you can remove the trigger from your life (for example, avoiding a bar if you're an alcoholic), you can evade the habit.

Unfortunately, triggering the habit is often unavoidable. For one thing, many habits are triggered by stress, and nobody lives a totally stress-free life. Once a habit is triggered, the only way to control it is through activation of the prefrontal cortex.

Our large prefrontal cortex is what separates us from other animals. Pretty much all other animals live their lives by impulse and routine, but we humans have the capability to overcome that through willful action. In this case, "willful" means we consciously and deliberately "put on the brakes" to stop acting out a habit. Willful actions are enacted by the prefrontal cortex, and inhibiting impulses requires proper serotonin function in the prefrontal cortex.

Unfortunately, you don't have an unlimited supply of serotonin. Each time you inhibit an impulse, it makes it harder to inhibit other impulses. Resisting impulses is like fighting an army of zombies with a limited number of bullets. Eventually you'll run out. Fortunately, there are remedies. You can create better habits, so that you don't have to rely on the prefrontal cortex, and you can boost your serotonin activity; we'll cover both in chapter 8.

Another solution is to make inhibiting your bad impulses and routines pleasurable in itself—and that becomes possible if you're inspired by a goal. Setting goals changes the activity in multiple brain regions, including the nucleus accumbens, prefrontal cortex, and anterior cingulate. We'll cover the power of setting goals in chapter 6.

Ultimately, it comes down to the most clichéd but scientifically true maxim: practice, practice, practice. To create new, good habits, you have to repeat them over and over again until your brain rewires itself. At the end of the day, repeating actions is the only way to get them encoded into the dorsal striatum. It may take a lot of time and patience, but once you train your dorsal striatum, it'll start working for you instead of against you; we'll cover that more in chapter 8. And it's pretty amazing that it's possible—no matter how old you are, you still have the power to change your brain and improve your life.

Conclusion of Part 1

So far we've learned how your brain circuits interact to create the downward spiral of depression. The prefrontal cortex worries too much, and the emotional limbic system is too reactive. The insula makes things feel worse, and the anterior cingulate isn't helping by focusing on the negative. On top of that, the prefrontal cortex has a hard time inhibiting the bad habits of the dorsal striatum and nucleus accumbens. Depression is so hard to overcome because each circuit pulls the others downward.

But there's good news. Your brain is not set in stone. Life changes cause brain changes—you can willfully change the activity, chemistry, and wiring of the regions and circuits in your brain that lead to depression. Like upgrading your computer, you can change not only the software but also the hardware. The changes are not always big, but they add up—each one pushing the brain toward an upward spiral.

And your upward spiral has already started simply by gaining a better understanding of depression. Understanding is powerful in itself, because knowing what's going on creates a better sense of control. Understanding also provides a step toward acceptance, and until you accept how things are now, it is difficult, if not impossible, to change.

Fortunately, neuroscience offers more than just understanding. Part 2 of this book contains many ways to change brain activity and chemistry to create an upward spiral: exercising (chapter 5), making decisions (chapter 6), improving your sleep (chapter 7), creating good habits (chapter 8), using your body (chapter 9), becoming more grateful (chapter 10), and relying on other people (chapter 11), as well as getting professional help (chapter 12). You don't have to change your life in all these areas to see a benefit; each small change in one area will benefit the others. So without further neuroscientific ado, let's get started.

Part 2

Creating an Upward Spiral

Chapter 5

Exercise Your Brain

A few years ago I got a new job at UCLA, and my boss bought me a laptop so I could work from anywhere. I was excited about not having to go in to the office. No need to dress up, no need to commute. I thought I might go to the park and work in the fresh air, or to a cool coffee shop. But I pretty much just sat on the couch in my dim living room. Around the same time, my girlfriend moved ninety miles up the coast. Fortunately, it was a beautiful drive, but it meant about three hours of extra driving every few days.

After a few weeks, I started getting a pain in my hip. Then my back started aching right between my shoulder blades. I felt both lazy and restless, but I didn't know what to do. I began to feel more sedentary, heavier, older. Food didn't taste as good, though I still ate plenty of it. It wasn't until several months later that I realized how inactive I had become.

I just didn't feel like exercising. Maybe you know the feeling. After sitting on the couch all day, I just wanted to keep sitting. My body felt uncomfortable, so I didn't feel like moving it around. Previously, when I had been going to UCLA every day, I used to go to the track or a yoga studio a few times a week. It was easy, because they were both right near work. But from the vantage point of the couch, it felt like too much effort to go running or yoga-ing. And the more out of shape I got, the more I lost interest in getting back in shape.

I'd been caught in a downward spiral and hadn't realized it. It's a bit silly that it started with a laptop, but there you go. In fact, that's usually how downward spirals start. A small change leads to unintended consequences that build on each other. We all know how important exercise is for your body, but what I didn't realize then is how important exercise is for your brain.

Your brain does not live in a jar, disconnected from the world. It is interconnected with your body, so the things you do with your body affect your neurochemistry. Your brain does not like being idle; it comes with a body, and it wants to use it.

This half of the book is about creating an upward spiral in which positive life changes cause positive brain changes, and vice versa. We're going to kick it off by talking about exercise. And by "exercise," I just mean moving around. It doesn't mean you need to go to the gym or buy fancy workout clothes; you just need to move your body more and not be so sedentary.

> **Have fun (a.k.a. don't "exercise").** When you don't think of it as "exercise" but rather as "being active" or "having fun," you're more likely to do it, and it will have a bigger emotional benefit. If you bike to work three days a week or play Frisbee with friends in the park, it won't feel like you're exercising, but it'll add up to a lot of activity.

Exercise is possibly the most straightforward and powerful way to start an upward spiral. Not only is it easy to understand, but exercise also has many of the same effects on the brain as antidepressant medications and even mimics the buzz of recreational drugs. Yet exercise is natural, it causes more nuanced and targeted brain changes, and its benefits can exceed even those of medication.

Don't Feel Like Exercising?

Of course you don't feel like exercising, but that's just your depressed brain circuits talking. Depression is a stable state, which means that your brain tends to think and act in ways that keep you depressed. To overcome depression, your brain needs to get off its lazy butt, and you've got to make it. Now I'm not calling *you* lazy; I'm calling *your brain* lazy. But at the end of the day, you're the one who can do something about it.

Do it with someone else. Not only is social interaction good for depression (chapter 11), but social pressure will also help you exercise. So ask a friend what type of activity he or she wants to get into, and join in. You could hire a trainer, attend a class, or join an exercise group. Having an accountability partner makes it more likely you'll show up.

What Exercise Does for You and Your Brain

I'm sure you've heard a million times how good exercise is for you. Well, now it's time to make it a million and one. Exercise is good for you. And not just for your heart and your waistline, but also for your brain—specifically, for the circuits that keep you depressed. Almost everything that depression causes can be combatted by exercise.

For example:

- Physically

    - Depression makes you lethargic and tired, but exercise gives you more energy and vitality.

- Depression often messes up your sleep patterns, but exercise improves your sleep, making it more restorative for your brain (chapter 7).

- Depression wreaks havoc on your appetite, so you either eat too little or chow down on junk food (in fact, people who eat lots of processed foods are at higher risk for depression[1]). Exercise improves your appetite, leading to more enjoyable eating and better health.

- Mentally

  - Depression can make it hard to concentrate, but exercise makes you mentally sharper and better at planning and decision making.[2]

  - Depression makes you…well…depressed, but exercise improves your mood.[3] It also reduces anxiety,[4] decreases stress,[5] and boosts self-esteem.

- Socially

  - Depression usually keeps you isolated and alone, but exercise tends to bring you out into the world.

Furthermore, all of these effects make it more likely that you'll engage in other activities and thought processes that also reverse the course of depression. For example, exercise improves sleep, which then reduces pain, improves mood, and increases energy and alertness. Then reduced pain makes you more likely to exercise and increases your enjoyment of exercise. Having more energy also makes it more likely that you'll exercise. The take-home message is that all these causes and effects intermingle and build on each other in an upward spiral toward feeling better.

Steroids for Your Brain

Just as exercise strengthens your muscles, it also strengthens your brain. Exercise increases nerve growth factors, such as brain-derived neurotrophic factor (BDNF), which are like steroids for your brain. BDNF makes your brain stronger, so it's more resistant to all kinds of problems, not only depression.[6]

Commit to a brief trial period. Sign up for an exercise class and commit to going to the first three. Check online sites like Groupon or LivingSocial for a monthlong trial to your local yoga or Pilates studio at a discounted rate. Join a gym and promise yourself that for the first two weeks you'll go every Monday, Wednesday, and Friday. Even if you're feeling too tired to do any actual exercise, still go to the gym, park your car, walk in, change into workout clothes, and pick up one five-pound weight. If you're really so tired that you don't want to do anything else there, that's totally fine. You've fulfilled your obligation to yourself (and to me), and you can go home and waste time on the Internet.

Numerous studies have demonstrated that exercise causes growth of new neurons. In one study, a pair of Texas scientists looked at the effects of exercise on rats.[7] The rats were divided into three groups: voluntary running, forced running, and controls. Those in the voluntary running group were allowed to run at whatever speed they felt like, while those in the forced group had to run at a set speed. The controls weren't allowed to run at all.

The study showed that both exercise groups had greater development of new neurons in the hippocampus. However, the voluntary group had more new neurons than the forced group, which suggests that actively choosing to exercise provides more benefits than being forced to. (We'll cover that kind of self-motivation in greater detail in chapter 6.) It also suggests that while hitting the treadmill at the gym might not be as great as running through the park, it's much better than doing nothing. And to start an upward spiral, all you need is something, no matter how small, that's better than what you're doing right now.

Enjoy the view. Exercising in pleasant environments, whether urban or rural—or while looking at images of pleasant environments—boosts the benefits of exercise.[8] In fact, irrespective of exercise, being in nature or even just looking at views of trees or lakes can have a big impact on your mood and can reduce depressive symptoms.[9] So try going for a run in a park, or pick a treadmill near a window.

Importantly, the benefits of neuron growth aren't evident just in rats; they're also in humans (like you). Neuron growth actually increases gray matter throughout the prefrontal cortex.[10] This exercise-induced BDNF increase is cool in itself, but it will seem even cooler when I tell you that BDNF is also increased by antidepressant medication, particularly in the frontal lobe.[11] Thus, exercise has an effect on the brain similar to that of antidepressants.

So once I got up off that couch and started walking, my brain started producing BDNF and growing stronger. I wasn't aware of it, but I had set a series of neural events in motion. But remember, BDNF is like fertilizer. You can't just sprinkle fertilizer on newly planted seeds and ask, "Now where are my plants?" It takes time. Exercise helps create the conditions for growth, but you've got to keep it up and give it time to work.

Pumping Up Your Serotonin

The relationship between exercise and antidepressants doesn't end with neuron-strengthening BDNF. Most antidepressants target the serotonin system and elevate serotonin levels, which increases motivation and willpower. Well, it turns out that exercise can also boost serotonin activity.[12]

Think about what's important to you. When you connect your exercise to a long-term goal, it helps your brain overlook momentary discomfort and makes your exercise more satisfying (chapter 6). In my case, I reminded myself that being in better shape made playing sports more fun. Maybe you'll do it for your kids. Maybe you'll do it because you value hard work. Only you know what's most important to you.

Movement increases the firing rate of serotonin neurons, which causes them to release more serotonin. And when more serotonin is released, more is produced to keep up with demand.[13] Notably, increased serotonin occurs with any movement, not just formal exercise, meaning that even vacuuming, gardening, or walking to a faraway parking spot will benefit your brain.

Importantly, serotonin and BDNF are particularly good at creating an upward spiral, because serotonin stimulates the production of BDNF, and BDNF strengthens serotonin neurons.[14] Exercise sets the snowball in motion, and the brain's dynamic interactions keep it going.

Energize Your Norepinephrine

The difficulties with concentration and deep thinking that often accompany depression are mainly the fault of a lagging norepinephrine system, which is why, next to serotonin, norepinephrine's the neurotransmitter most commonly targeted by antidepressant medications. Fortunately, exercise increases norepinephrine as well.[15] A study in Germany had subjects either rest, jog slowly, or sprint at high speed. While all exercise increased norepinephrine, intense exercise was particularly helpful. So if you can find the energy to push yourself, your brain will make it worth your while.

Reward Yourself with Dopamine

Dopamine is your brain's version of methamphetamines. The dopamine circuit in the brain controls aspects of pleasure, decision making, and focus. It's the primary neurotransmitter behind addiction. All those addictive drugs called "uppers," like crystal meth or cocaine, are basically jacking up your dopamine. In fact, any addiction—not just to drugs, but also to risk taking, emotional drama, or whatever turns you on—simply hijacks the brain's natural capacity to enjoy things. Dysfunctional dopamine explains the lack of enjoyment that often accompanies depression. Fortunately—you guessed it—the dopamine system is also positively affected by exercise.[16]

Exercise before you reward yourself. Let's face it: you're going to watch television. You're going to eat ice cream. You're going to waste time on Facebook. No big deal. But the next time you do, make it a reward for something. Exercise beforehand. Walk up and down the stairs twice. Do ten sit-ups. Jog around the block. You were going to have the reward anyway, so just insert a little activity into your inactivity. And when you feel that you earned that television show or that ice cream, it's even more enjoyable.

A group of British scientists examined cigarette cravings in smokers before and after exercise.[17] After not being allowed to smoke for fifteen hours, the participants were divided into two groups: an exercise group and a control group. The exercise group got on a stationary bike for ten minutes and pedaled at a light to moderate intensity, while the control group just sat there.

When subsequently examined in a functional MRI scan, the control group had a predictable brain response to looking at cigarettes. They showed increased activity in the *orbitofrontal cortex*, which is part of the ventral prefrontal cortex and is involved with motivation. They also showed significant activation in the dorsal striatum. Both of these regions are influenced by dopamine activity. In other words, their brains *really* wanted those cigarettes and were activating habits to do something about it.

> **Keep an exercise plan.** Add exercise on your to-do list or calendar and check it off when you complete it. Planning activates the prefrontal cortex, and checking it off the list releases dopamine. Win-win.

On the other hand, the exercise group had a different brain response to looking at cigarettes. Remember the two groups were exactly the same except for a ten-minute period of exercise. And yet after biking, the exercise group showed decreased activity in those brain areas—their brains wanted the cigarettes less. Just ten minutes of exercise had significantly altered their dopamine circuits and increased their willpower. Yes, pedaling a couple miles on a stationary bike while reading the latest issue of *People* won't solve all your problems, but for your brain, it's a heckuva lot better than just sitting there, and it's a great kick start to an upward spiral.

The Runner's High

Natural neurochemicals or illegal street drugs? Sometimes it's hard to tell. Exercise causes your brain to release *endorphins*, neurotransmitters that act on your neurons like opiates (such as morphine or Vicodin) by sending a neural signal to reduce pain and provide anxiety relief.

A group of German scientists used positron emission tomography (a PET scan) to look at changes in endorphin activity after exercise.[18] They found that exercise increased endorphins in the brain and that these changes correlated with improving people's mood. And there were significant correlations in several key areas, including the orbitofrontal cortex, the dorsolateral prefrontal cortex, the insula, and the anterior cingulate.

You may remember from part 1 that these areas, as key players in frontal-limbic circuitry, are important in contributing to depression. The orbitofrontal cortex influences motivation and decision making. The dorsolateral prefrontal cortex helps with planning and thinking. The insula modulates pain perception. And the anterior cingulate guides your focus. Amazingly, endorphin signaling in all of these areas is improved by exercise.

Endorphin release is highest during intense exercise.[19] So if you can manage to push yourself through a hard workout, you'll get a bigger endorphin boost. But if you can't get the runner's high, it's fine to settle for the walker's buzz.

Opiates aren't the only class of recreational drugs your brain can mimic. Exercise also increases activation of the *endocannabinoid* system.[20] You may not have heard of endocannabinoids before, but they are a naturally occurring chemical in your brain that was named after cannabis (marijuana). The active ingredient in marijuana (tetrahydrocannabinol, or THC) activates this same system, causing reduced pain sensitivity and an improved sense of well-being. That's one of the reasons exercise reduces pain and increases positive feelings (and may contribute to the munchies).

Calming Your Stress Hormones

The relationship between stress and depression is a two-way street: depression is stressful, and stress pushes you toward depression. Yes, it's another freakin' downward spiral. Luckily, exercise can help.

Make it simple. It's much easier to convince yourself to do simple, easy activities. Try starting with one push-up after you check your email in the morning. If you start feeling better and want to do more, go for it. But if all you ever do is one push-up, that's better than nothing.

A collaboration of Japanese and Thai researchers looked at the effects of exercise on stress in a group of depressive teenage girls. The researchers had the girls either join an exercise class every weekday for eight weeks or just do their normal activities. The study showed that exercise dramatically reduced their stress hormones (such as, cortisol and adrenaline) and depression, and improved their physical health and social relationships.[21] This exemplifies the upward spiral: one life change can have multiple, seemingly unrelated effects.

Increasing Blood Flow in the Prefrontal Cortex

While most neuroscience studies compare brain activity before and after exercise, a group of researchers in Tokyo wanted to look at brain activity *during* exercise.[22] They had to use *near infrared spectroscopy*, a technology that can see changes in blood flow even through the skull. While subjects pedaled on a stationary bike (scientists are just really into stationary bikes), they experienced increases in oxygenated blood in the ventral prefrontal cortex, accompanied by improved moods and increased energy levels.

Sitting is the new smoking. In other words, it's bad for you. If you sit at a computer all day (like me), get up and walk around at least once every hour. And every twenty minutes, briefly stretch your hands, arms, and back. Try working at a standing desk or replace your chair with an exercise ball. Walk while you're on the phone.

A Better Night's Sleep

Considering that you spend a third of your life asleep (or at least trying to fall asleep), changes in sleep patterns can have a huge impact on the rest of your life.

A group of researchers at Northwestern University divided adults with insomnia into two groups.[23] One group was instructed to exercise at a moderate intensity four days a week, while the other group did other fun things, like taking cooking classes or going to a museum. After four months, the people in the exercise group fell asleep faster and slept longer than the others. They also had improved mood, more energy, and an overall better quality of life. That's one of the interesting things about exercise. When you start doing it, you might be more tired, but after a while, you end up with more energy overall to do other fun things.

So what exactly is happening in the brain when it is sleeping? You might be aware that your brain goes through different phases while it's asleep, and you've probably heard of one sleep phase, *REM sleep*, which stands for rapid eye movement. In REM sleep, your brain is a lot more active than in other phases of sleep. We'll go into this more in chapter 7, but basically, people with depression show increased amounts of REM sleep, which means their sleep is not as restful.[24] Antidepressant medications reduce REM sleep,[25] as does exercise. So…exercise, sleep more deeply, feel happier and more energetic, want to exercise more, rinse, repeat.

An Upward Exercise Spiral

So there I was working on the couch or sitting in traffic, aching and aging and out of shape. Around that time, my roommate started training for the LA Marathon and tried to convince me to join him. I didn't think there was any way I could run a marathon, but seeing his energy and eagerness helped me finally recognize the downward spiral I'd gotten into. So I started making some small changes.

After eating breakfast, I would go for a short walk. I didn't plan it; I just walked out the door and meandered around a few blocks, soaking in the sun. And even though I didn't have to, I started going to the office anyway. That meant walking to the car, from the parking lot to the building, and up some stairs. It also made me less isolated and closer to the track and the yoga studio, increasing the likelihood I would actually work out. Lastly, I made a more concerted effort to play sports, which is not only physical and social but fun too.

With each little bit of exercise I did, each time I chose to move a little more, everything became easier. My brain was juicing up on all those good neurochemicals—all that serotonin, dopamine, and norepinephrine began making things happen. The BDNF was silently working away. As a result, not only did I have a bigger appetite, but food tasted better, and I wanted to eat healthier foods. I didn't worry about things as much, and my sleep improved. I felt like I had more free time and even felt younger. Then exercise became more appealing, and slowly I became intrigued by the thought of a marathon.

That highlights an important part of the upward spiral: once you get things going, it becomes self-sustaining. Yes, you often need to give it a few pushes, but you'll be surprised sometimes by how your brain just starts to make things easier all on its own. While I hadn't liked distance running before, I found after a few slow jogs that I enjoyed the simple freedom of stepping out of my door and going. I didn't need to go to a gym. I didn't need to coordinate with friends. I could just run.

Creating Your Own Upward Spiral

One of the greatest obstacles to exercise is that people with depression don't feel like doing it. Thinking about exercise is often accompanied by automatic negative thoughts like *Oh, that's not gonna help*. But that's just because the depressed brain is stuck in a depressed loop and doesn't know how to get out.

> **Make an anti-laziness rule.** Decide ahead of time that you'll take the stairs for anything less than three floors. Decide that you'll walk to do any errand that is less than a mile away or bike to any that are less than two miles away. Commit to never taking an escalator if the stairs are right next to it. Don't circle the parking lot looking for a closer space, just take the first one you see.

There is no one solution. There are only parts of the solution. You don't need to do everything. Any little thing you do is a step in the right direction. Every minute you walk instead of sitting on the couch is a jump start to an upward spiral.

Remember that even if it doesn't feel like the exercise is working, it's still causing tons of unnoticed brain changes. It's modifying circuits, releasing positive neurochemicals, and reducing stress hormones. So stop worrying about whether each step will make you feel better. Stop asking, *Am I feeling better yet?* Just absorb yourself in the task of living your life.

You might think, *I already tried that, and it didn't work.* But in complex systems like the brain, the same actions can cause different reactions at different times in your life. It's like traffic changes— during Friday rush hour, road construction might cause a traffic jam, but on a Saturday, the same construction might barely slow anyone down. Just because something didn't help at one point in your life does not mean it will never help.

"But I can't…" is a common objection to exercise. "But I can't go to the gym three times a week." So go to the gym once a week. "But I can't run a marathon." So run a mile. "But I can't run." So walk. Once you stop focusing on all the things you can't do, you may start to be amazed by what you *can* do.

Your depressed brain might be telling you to give up. It might be telling you that everything hurts too much to exercise. Thank it for its opinion, and go for a walk.

Chapter 6

Set Goals, Make Decisions

In the nonfiction mountain-climbing classic *Touching the Void*, two explorers, Joe Simpson and Simon Yates, attempt a first ascent of the west face of Siula Grande in the Peruvian Andes. Spoiler alert: it's a tough climb, but they make it to the top. The real story starts on their way down. A storm sets in, battering and blinding them, and in the turmoil, Joe falls and breaks his leg. With just the two of them—in the middle of a storm, and night quickly approaching—the prospects look grim. They don't know what to do or the best way down. If Simon tries to carry Joe, they might both end up dying. Joe can't see any way out for himself and thinks this is the end. (Spoiler alert #2: it's not, because he's the author of the book.) It's at this point in the book that Joe explains an important aspect of surviving in the wilderness, "You gotta keep making decisions, even if they're wrong decisions, you know. If you don't make decisions, you're stuffed."

In mountaineering, if you're stuck in a bad situation and you don't know the right way out, you just have to pick a direction and go. It doesn't have to be the best direction; there may not even be a best direction. You certainly don't have enough information to know for sure. So if you start down a path and end up at a cliff, you'll just have to pick another direction from there. Because guess what? In a dire situation, you can't be certain of the right path; what you do know is that if you sit there and do nothing, you're screwed.

Perhaps that is like the situation you find yourself in. Every decision feels wrong. But that's just because your limbic system is overwhelming your prefrontal cortex. It is a symptom of depression. In fact, it's one of the symptoms that makes depression so stable. If you could be decisive, then you would start living your life boldly instead of tentatively. But you can't.

Make a good decision, not the best decision. When trying to make a decision, we tend to focus on the relative drawbacks of each option, which often makes every decision seem less appealing.[1] Nor do we usually have enough information to feel confident in the decision—the world's just too complex. But remember, it's better to do something only partly right than do nothing at all. Trying for the best, instead of good enough, brings too much emotional ventromedial prefrontal activity into the decision-making process.[2] In contrast, recognizing that good enough is good enough activates more dorsolateral prefrontal areas, which helps you feel more in control.

Making decisions includes creating intentions and setting goals—all three are part of the same neural circuitry and engage the prefrontal cortex in a positive way, reducing worry and anxiety. Making decisions also helps overcome striatum activity, which usually pulls you toward negative impulses and routines. Finally, making decisions changes your perception of the world—finding solutions to your problems and calming your limbic system.

Why Decisions Aren't Easy

Have people told you that your indecisiveness gets in the way of your happiness? Before you get too upset with yourself about this, remember that being indecisive stems from caring too much about too many things. If you cared about only one thing, it would be easy to be decisive, but your personality and your brain are more complex and nuanced than that. Since your actions are guided by the dynamic interaction of your striatum, limbic system, and prefrontal cortex, your goals, habits, fears, and desires all compete for limited brain resources. Sometimes the communication between these brain areas reaches a stalemate, and you get stuck on a decision. And sometimes you get stuck on *every* decision, which is when indecisiveness gets in your way. It can affect your anxiety, mood, thoughts, and actions—all of which, unfortunately, fuels further indecisiveness.

So why does decision making (or the lack thereof) have such a profound effect on your life? The answer, of course, can be found inside the brain, and it starts with the prefrontal cortex.

Deciding Engages the Prefrontal Cortex

Your brain, like your muscles, operates on a use-it-or-lose-it basis. Using a particular brain region will strengthen it, while disuse will weaken it. One problem with depression is that it makes you use a lot of the brain circuits that keep you stuck and less of the brain circuits that help you get better. Decision making is a great way to start an upward spiral, because it engages a circuit that helps you get better. Intentional, goal-directed decisions require the use of the prefrontal cortex, specifically the *ventromedial prefrontal cortex*,[3] which helps rebalance the dysfunctional frontal-limbic circuitry.

Take a step in the right direction. Confucius said that "The journey of a thousand miles begins with a single step," and this is certainly true with the brain. You start by making a decision in your head, but the decision-making process isn't complete until you take a step in that direction. Conversely, a trip to the supermarket or finishing that report for work might feel like a thousand-mile journey, but all you have to do is take one tiny step in the direction of that goal. Write down one thing you want at the supermarket, or start by looking for your car keys. A decision without action is just a thought, and while thoughts can be helpful, they won't have as powerful an impact on your brain. A decision with action is something else entirely: it's a robust way to start an upward spiral.

In general, the prefrontal cortex is responsible for *goal-directed behavior*. That means it decides what goals to achieve and how to achieve them, and the first step to achieving goals is all about making decisions. Once a decision is made, the prefrontal cortex organizes your actions to achieve that goal. It accomplishes this by more effectively managing the resources the brain has at its disposal.

Deciding Focuses Attention and Enhances Perception

In the complex world we live in, there's a lot of irrelevant information (advertisements, noise, how your stomach feels, the weather, and so forth). When you make a decision, the prefrontal cortex helps you ignore irrelevant distractions and focus on completing a goal.

We've all heard the idea that we use only 10 percent of our brains...and it's a big fat lie. Everyone uses their whole brain, although when your brain is processing too many irrelevancies, it loses power to process the things that are most important to you. Fortunately, one of the most important consequences of decision making is that it helps reshape your brain's perception and guides its attention to the things that matter most—just as Google biases your search results toward the most important. If the important results were buried on page 25, you'd never see them.

When you decide on a goal, the prefrontal cortex changes the way the rest of the brain perceives the world. That doesn't sound profound enough—when you decide on a goal, the prefrontal cortex changes the way you see and smell and hear the world in front of you. Decision making in the prefrontal cortex, which is a high-level brain process, affects the lower-level sensory processes.

Every sense you have has a *sensory cortex* devoted to it. You have a visual cortex and an auditory cortex and so forth. These lower-level sensory cortices are under *top-down control*. The prefrontal cortex can tell the lower-level cortices what to ignore and what to pay attention to. It's like a chief of police telling the department, "Ignore speeding tickets; catch drug dealers." If you spend your brain's resources looking for something particular, you're more likely to find it.

In your current situation, it might seem like there are no solutions to your problems, but the solutions are there; you just can't see them, because you're overwhelmed by irrelevant details. Top-down control suppresses the lower-level cortex response to irrelevant information and enhances both the speed and amount of activation for important information.[4] For example, when looking for your car keys, the reactivity of your visual cortex is enhanced. Maybe that doesn't sound spectacular, but it's like the feature on new cameras that highlights faces. Whenever a face enters the picture, the camera puts a little square around it and focuses on it. Imagine if you could do that for everything—if a little box suddenly appeared around your car keys when you needed them. Or if you were looking to strengthen your relationship with your spouse, and suddenly you saw a way to do just that. Once you make a decision and create an intention to solve a specific problem, the potential solutions are highlighted in the brain in a similar way.

Figure out what's important to you. To help reduce irrelevant details in your life, focus on what's really important to you. Studies have found that focusing on your values reduces the brain's stress response.[5] So think about the times in your life when you were happiest. What were you doing then, and what factors contributed to your happiness? What activities make you feel most fulfilled? What achievements are you most proud of? What good qualities would you want coworkers or friends to use in describing you?

Top-down control was beautifully illustrated in one clever study in which participants were asked periodically to point at a cup, grab it, or do nothing. (Yes, this is a very simple goal, but you too should start with simple goals.) After being told which action to make, but before doing it, participants were presented with images of circles, and their job was to find the one that didn't match the rest. Sometimes the non-matching circle was brighter than the rest, and at other times it was smaller. Amazingly, the intention to either point at or grab the cup changed the way participants perceived the circles. When they were preparing to point, it was easier for them to find bright circles; when they were preparing to grab, it was easier to find smaller circles. The intended action caused differences both in their reaction times and in the electrical activity of the visual cortex itself.[6] Finally, when asked to do nothing—and thus having no intention to reach or grab—participants' visual cortex responded equally to both types of circles. This study may seem strange, but it proves that making a decision changes your brain's perceptual processing of the world.

Of course, changing the way your brain perceives the world is not going to solve all your problems. Imagine you're trying to find your car keys in the dark. Turning on the light will not magically reveal them—maybe they're in the pants you were wearing yesterday or under the couch cushions. But turning on the light will sure as heck improve your chances of finding them. Making a decision, even a tiny decision, starts shedding light on ways to improve your life.

Deciding Increases Enjoyment

We are often under the impression that we are happy when good things happen to us. But in actuality, we are happiest when we decide to pursue a particular goal and then achieve it. One big problem with depression is that in the short term, nothing feels pleasurable. Because of frontal-limbic miscommunications, you can't connect future happiness to today's actions. Thus any action that isn't immediately pleasurable becomes difficult.

Actively choosing to pursue a goal, however, rather than relying on impulse or habit, makes it more rewarding. For example, in one study, rats were paired up to receive injections of cocaine. Rat A could press a lever to receive cocaine, and rat B just had to wait until rat A pressed the lever. So they both got the same injections of cocaine at the same time, but rat A had to actively press the lever, and rat B didn't have to do anything.[7] And you guessed it—rat A released more dopamine in its nucleus accumbens. So deciding on a goal and then achieving it feels more rewarding than if something good happens to you by chance. Sure, giving cocaine to rats may not be the most uplifting example, but the same processes apply to other things. If you decide to buy a cookie, it will be more enjoyable than if someone hands you a cookie. If you decide to pursue a job, it will be more rewarding than if someone offers it to you out of the blue. If you decide to get out of bed, it will be more empowering than waiting until you have to go to the bathroom.

Decide for something you want, not against something you don't want. Focusing on potential negative outcomes makes decision making more difficult.[8] Actively choosing a particular goal you want to pursue—rather than basing your decision on avoiding something you don't want—forces you to focus on the positive, at least briefly. For example, instead of "I don't want to do a bad job," say, "I want to do a great job." This type of positive thinking is more effective at changing your behavior.[9]

In another study—this one on humans—participants played a gambling game. In one part of the study, they actively chose how much to bet, and in the other, a computer chose for them. For the most part, their brains had a predictable response to winning money, regardless of who decided to make the bet—with one important exception. When the participants decided how much to bet, their brains showed greater activity in the anterior cingulate, insula, striatum, and hippocampus. Activity in these regions says that deciding for yourself is associated with greater importance placed on winning, more emotional engagement, more likely changes in behavior, and enhanced memory.[10]

In another fMRI study, participants played a different type of gambling game, one in which they had to inflate a computerized balloon.[11] As the balloon got bigger and bigger, it had a greater likelihood of popping. They could choose to inflate it a little more to win increasing amounts of money. However, in other parts of the study, the choice was taken out of their hands, and the computer chose for them. When choosing for themselves, participants had more activation in the dorsal anterior cingulate, the insula, and the nucleus accumbens. Actively choosing caused changes in attention circuits and in how the participants felt about the action, and it increased rewarding dopamine activity.

Here's one more. In a classic study of choice, a team at Harvard asked subjects to rank a set of paintings in order of preference.[12] Then the subjects were presented with pairs of paintings and asked which one they would like to hang in their own home. Later the subjects were asked to rank the paintings again. Actively choosing a painting they would like in their own home caused its preference rank to go up, and actively rejecting a painting caused its preference rank to go down. This effect was seen even when subjects had amnesia and could not remember which paintings they chose. The simple act of choosing had an effect deeper than conscious memory. We don't just choose the things we like; we also like the things we choose.

Setting Goals to Increase Dopamine

People are often at their best when working toward a long-term, meaningful goal that they believe is achievable, like earning a degree or getting a promotion. That's because not only is dopamine released when you finally achieve a long-term goal but it's also released with each step you make as you move closer to achieving it. Having a goal also allows the prefrontal cortex to more effectively organize your actions. And most importantly, achieving the goal is often less important to happiness than setting the goal in the first place.[13]

Unfortunately, people with depression tend to create nebulous goals that are poorly defined, which makes progress and achievement difficult.[14] For example, a nebulous goal might be "Spend more time with my kids," whereas "Play board games with my kids every Sunday" is a specific one. When goals are poorly defined, it becomes difficult for the brain to determine whether you've actually accomplished them or are even moving toward them. Not only does that mean less dopamine, but the lack of perceived progress can be de-motivating.

On top of that, not believing you can achieve your goals increases feelings of hopelessness.[15] Thus, it's important to have at least a few goals that you believe you can achieve. Creating specific, meaningful, and achievable long-term goals can be a powerful way to reverse the course of depression.

Create specific long-term goals. Start by thinking about your values and what's important to you. Write down at least one or two specific goals that you could achieve that align with what's important to you. A specific goal has a clearly defined benchmark of success, so at some point in the future you will know definitively whether or not you have achieved it. Do the goals on your list inspire or motivate you? If not, think harder about some different goals.

If you have found some specific, meaningful goals, do you believe you can achieve any of them? If not, break them down into smaller goals that you believe may be achievable. For example, if the goal of finding a job seems too daunting, try setting a smaller goal of sending out two resumes a week, or spending ten minutes every day look for a job online.

Deciding Can Both Override or Utilize Habits

As I discussed in chapter 4, most of your actions are driven by routine or impulse. You're basically on autopilot most of the time, guided by the dorsal striatum or the nucleus accumbens. Pretty much the only way to override a programmed routine or suppress an impulse is to make a decision with the prefrontal cortex.

Importantly, the medial prefrontal cortex *projects to* the dorsal striatum, and the orbitofrontal cortex *projects to* the nucleus accumbens.[16] That may sound like gibberish, but it means that the prefrontal cortex is able to modulate your habits and impulses. That gives you more control over your own life so that you're not controlled solely by your past experiences or current environment.

In addition to utilizing the prefrontal cortex to suppress bad habits, you can use it to activate good habits (further explained in chapter 8). If you have a good habit you're trying to develop, but which isn't ingrained yet, it's wired weakly in the dorsal striatum, waiting to be triggered. The good news is that the prefrontal cortex can trigger that good habit and strengthen its wiring. There's nothing wrong with being on autopilot and letting the habits in the dorsal striatum take over, as long as you first make sure you're headed in the right direction.

Deciding Creates Perceived Control

You may not make all the right decisions, but they will be *your* decisions. And the mammalian brain works much better when it has some control over the world than when it doesn't. Indecisiveness is part of the downward spiral because it enhances your feeling of being out of control.

The best examples of this come from experiments on uncontrollable stress. In one study, rats are placed in pairs and given small, but random, shocks on the tail.[17] Their tails are connected by a wire, so they experience the same shocks. When a shock comes on, rat A can spin a wheel and make it stop for both rats. Rat B also has a wheel, but unfortunately, it's not connected to anything; it just has to wait for rat A to stop the shocks. Interestingly, even though both rats receive the same random shocks—at the same time and for the same duration—after the experiment, rat A ends up pretty well off, but rat B develops symptoms of depression. And in fact, rat B, who had no control, has lower dopamine and norepinephrine in the frontal lobe and lower serotonin in the brain stem. The amount that you feel in control of a situation lowers your stress level.

A group of British researchers conducted a human fMRI experiment that was similar to the rat experiment. Subjects were hooked up with electrodes on their hands and shocked randomly. In one part of the experiment, they could press a button to stop the shock, but in other parts, the shocks were ended by a computer. Having control over the shock reduced the amount of reactivity in brain pain circuits,[18] and it increased activity in the dorsolateral prefrontal cortex and anterior cingulate. Interestingly, the more medial prefrontal activity subjects had, the less pain they experienced. This means that using decision making to increase medial prefrontal activity seems like a good idea.

You don't even need direct control over the cause of your stress to gain the benefits of decision making. As long as you have control over something, you can take advantage of the benefits. For example, when rats are exposed to uncontrollable stress, if they are given the choice to run on an exercise wheel, they don't suffer negative consequences.[19] Interestingly, if they are forced to exercise, they don't get the same benefits, because without choice, the exercise is itself a source of stress.[20] Obviously, exercise itself is important, as we covered in the last chapter, but *deciding* to exercise is also a powerful way to start an upward spiral.

The important thing here is not actual control, but perceived control. Making decisions may not increase your actual control over a situation, but it will likely increase your perceived control. And when you increase your perceived control, you increase your confidence, mood, and future decision-making capabilities.

Deciding Reduces Worry and Anxiety

As I explained in chapter 2, worry and anxiety are triggered by possibility, not certainty. When your prefrontal cortex has to loop through many potential scenarios, it increases the risk of triggering anxiety or worry. When you decide on one path, then you've reduced the number of variables the prefrontal cortex needs to optimize.

A decision is simply creating an intention to move in a particular direction. It doesn't mean that you need to go that direction forever. Imagine you're in the wilderness, like the two mountain climbers discussed at the beginning of this chapter, and you come to a fork in the path. You could spend forever trying to figure out which way to go, or you could pick one and go down it. You may eventually realize it's the wrong one—and if so, you turn around and end up back at the fork. Given the fact that you're back where you started, you might be tempted to think that was all wasted effort, but it wasn't. Going one way and then realizing you need to change course is different from just sitting there doing nothing. Even if your initial decision turns out to be wrong, you're still in control of your life.

One study demonstrated this by examining people with career indecisiveness. Everyone in the study was having trouble picking a career path. The researchers divided the participants into two groups—one studied a workbook that helped participants address their negative thoughts, while the other researched a career they were interested in. Both interventions reduced negative thoughts and anxiety, and both improved decisiveness.[21]

This study shows that working to reduce your focus on negative outcomes can help with decisiveness. But it also shows that simply picking a path has the same effect. The participants in the second group didn't need to choose the career they were going to end up with; they just took one step in a decisive direction, which reduced their future options and thus their anxiety.

Deciding Helps Make More Decisions

As I neared the end of college, I had a hard time deciding what I wanted to do with my life. This indecisiveness became insidious—soon I was having trouble deciding what I wanted to do for the summer, and then simply what I wanted to do that weekend.

When you're stalled and paralyzed, things feel out of your control. But the good news is that you don't have to start with the big decisions. You can start small. Choose what to have for lunch, or what television show to watch. Research shows that decisiveness in one part of your life can improve your decisiveness in other parts of your life.[22] Pick one thing, go with it, and don't question it.

When you exercise a muscle, it gets stronger, and the exercise makes it easier to work out the next time. Similarly, every time you make a decision instead of procrastinating, worrying, or acting impulsively, you strengthen your decision-making circuit for the future. Of course, if you run five miles, your muscles become fatigued, and a sixth mile is going to feel a lot harder than the first. The same with decisions—if you have to make a lot in a row, the decision-making circuit gets fatigued and your brain falls back into indecisiveness or impulsivity. But that's okay. Just like with exercise, you're training your brain for the future, and the next time you need to make a decision, that sixth mile will feel easier—you'll have set the stage for an upward spiral.

Chapter 7

Give Your Brain a Rest

I spent the summer of my junior year of college working in a sleep lab, which we called "Sleep Camp." Teenagers stayed in the lab for three weeks straight, while we studied their sleep patterns, hormone levels, and brain waves under tightly controlled conditions.

While it was a fascinating summer job, it wasn't very relaxing; the great irony of studying sleep is that you hardly get any sleep yourself. The lab needed to be staffed twenty-four hours a day, and I had the shift from 3:30 a.m. to noon. While the New England summer sun didn't set until past nine, I had to start getting ready for bed by eight thirty, and that only gave me six hours of sleep. Unfortunately, since I'd been studying the neuroscience of sleep, the worst part of having such a poor sleep schedule was that I was acutely aware of all its negative effects.

So why am I bringing this up now? Poor sleep is one of the most common symptoms of depression, as well as one of the biggest contributors to developing depression and staying depressed. And by "poor sleep," I mean getting not only too little sleep but also getting low-quality sleep. Mentally, poor sleep worsens your mood, lowers your pain threshold, and interferes with learning and memory. It also diminishes your ability to concentrate and makes you more impulsive. Physically, it increases blood pressure, elevates stress, and harms the immune system. It can even cause weight gain.

Poor sleep also has numerous negative effects on the brain, particularly in the prefrontal cortex and hippocampus. It also alters the function of the serotonin, dopamine, and norepinephrine systems. Fortunately, several large recent studies have shown that it is possible to greatly improve your sleep, which can dramatically relieve depression or even prevent it in the first place.

The key for improving your sleep comes down to two main factors: dealing with your anxieties and stress and improving your sleep hygiene. What is sleep hygiene? I'm glad you asked.

What Is Sleep Hygiene?

Sleep hygiene is the combination of your actions and the environment that precedes sleep or potentially interferes with it, including your bedtime routine, or lack thereof, as well as the level of noise and light in your bedroom. It also includes the time you go to sleep and wake up, and the amount of light and exercise you get during the day. Most problems with sleep are exacerbated by poor sleep hygiene, and some are caused entirely by it.

Good sleep hygiene is like good dental hygiene. If you take good care of your teeth, you probably won't get cavities, but it's not a guarantee. Some people could brush and floss three times a day and still have cavities, and other people could hardly ever brush and still be fine. But even with individual variability, it's certainly true that with bad dental hygiene, your teeth will be worse off. The same is true of sleep. Furthermore, your sleep needs change over the course of your lifetime—just because you could pull all-nighters in college with no problem doesn't mean your brain is still as amenable to poor sleep in the present. If you have any problems with sleep, they can most often be fixed with changes in sleep hygiene.

Neuroscience Basics of Sleep

"Sleep" is actually a blanket term (no pun intended) that covers numerous subtypes of sleep; all organized together, they create a *sleep architecture*, which is the first step to understanding sleep. Another important part of the sleep story, though it actually has nothing to do with sleeping, is your brain's internal clock—its *circadian rhythms*—which controls a variety of hormones and neurotransmitters on a daily cycle. If you can understand sleep architecture and circadian rhythms, you'll have a pretty good understanding of how sleep affects the brain.

Sleep Architecture

Most of us think of sleep as this big waste of time, when our brain doesn't do much. But in fact, sleep has an intricate architecture that is affected by our waking lives. And in a great example of an upward spiral, the quality of our sleep in turn affects our quality of life.

As I mentioned in chapter 5, your brain cycles through several different stages of sleep. When you first nod off, your brain enters stage 1, a very light sleep, when your brain's electrical waves begin to slow down. Interestingly, since stage 1 sleep is so light, many people with sleep problems often enter stage 1 sleep and then wake up without realizing they'd fallen asleep at all.[1] The misperception of having lain there awake the whole time adds to their distress.

After about five to ten minutes of stage 1 sleep, your brain goes deeper, into stage 2, then over the next hour, it progresses deeper into stages 3 and 4, in which your brain's electrical activity slows down dramatically. Because of the dramatic slowing, stages 3 and 4 are often called *slow-wave sleep*.

After slow-wave sleep comes REM sleep, in which your brain is a lot more active. As I mentioned in chapter 5, people with depression show increased amounts of REM sleep,[2] and they spend less time in slow-wave sleep, which means their sleep is less restful. One of the effects of antidepressant medications is to reduce REM sleep.[3]

One sleep cycle (in other words, one loop through all the stages) takes about ninety minutes. Then it starts again at stage 1. Your brain goes through the stages sequentially, just like a video game with different levels: 1 to 2 to 3 to 4 to REM. If you are woken up during stage 4, you start over again at stage 1. So if you don't sleep continuously, the proper progression is disrupted, and your sleep is less restorative. Interestingly, if you wake up during stage 1, you feel a lot more rested than if you are disturbed in other stages. You can actually buy a brain-wave alarm clock or app that will wake you in stage 1 (just look online). But in fact, if you wake up at the same time every day, your brain does this naturally.

Circadian Rhythms

The quality of your sleep is also affected by daily chemical fluctuations called *circadian rhythms*, which are governed by the hypothalamus and control a large number of processes, including hunger, alertness, and body temperature. Circadian rhythms also cause a variety of daily neurohormone fluctuations, including testosterone, cortisol, and melatonin.

If you were to live in complete darkness, your brain would still fluctuate with its natural rhythm of about twenty-four hours. In normal life, however, circadian rhythms don't run continuously on their twenty-four-hour cycle; they're kept synchronized to the daytime by the sun or bright lights. You have neurons that connect your eyeballs to your hypothalamus that reset your circadian clock every day.

> **Avoid bright lights after the sun goes down.** You don't need to walk around in the dark, but when it's getting close to bedtime, turn off most of the lights in your house. Turn down the brightness on your computer monitor or, better yet, don't stare at a screen at all. And make sure your bedroom is really dark when you're trying to sleep. If you've got several electronic devices in your bedroom that have LED lights, they can make enough light to disrupt your sleep. Move them to another room or cover the LEDs.

Sleep quality is best when your sleeping schedule is synchronized with your circadian rhythms. Unfortunately, there are many ways modern society can knock us out of that synchronization. The first is by looking at bright light at the wrong time. After the sun sets, your circadian rhythms tell your brain that it's nighttime and that it should start getting ready for sleep. But if you turn on bright lights, your brain thinks it's still daytime (after all, it evolved long before the lightbulb), and your circadian rhythms are shifted. Many light sources can shift the circadian cycle, including lamps, television screens, computers—even your iPhone.

A second way your circadian rhythms can be desynchronized is through changes in your bedtime. Your brain expects to go to sleep at a specific "time" of your circadian clock. The hypothalamus tells the rest of your brain that it's bedtime by triggering the release of the neurotransmitter melatonin (not to be confused with melanin in the skin, which affects skin color). Melatonin prepares your brain for sleep, just as jogging to warm up your muscles prepares your body for a strenuous workout (or coffee prepares you to do anything at all). When you change your usual bedtime, your brain isn't properly prepared for sleep. You might get the right amount of sleep, but the quality of that sleep will be diminished. Unfortunately, you can't set your brain clock like an alarm clock. Your brain is like a dog. It needs to be trained, and that requires repetition. It's okay to vary a little and also okay to occasionally stay up late, but there should be a clear time you think of as your bedtime. And yes, try to stick to it on weekends.

What Sleep Does for You

After a century of modern sleep research, the exact purpose of sleep is still a bit of a mystery. What we do know is that bad things happen if you don't get enough quality sleep and that improving the quality of your sleep can have profound benefits.

Sleep improves many aspects of waking life; it elevates mood, lowers stress, strengthens memory, and reduces pain. It also helps with concentration, thinking clearly, and decision making. The benefits of quality sleep even extend to your overall health. Poor sleep has negative effects on your weight, your heart, and even your immune system.[4] Sleep disturbances also increase the risk of drug or alcohol addiction.[5] Thus, if your depression is related to an underlying health or addiction problem, improving sleep is a great start to an upward spiral.

What Sleep Does for Your Brain

So how does sleep cause so many life changes? Because your brain's entire electrical and chemical activity is affected by sleep.

Sleep and Clear Thinking

Many people with depression have difficulty thinking clearly and being decisive, and these problems are exacerbated by sleep problems.[6] After a bad night of sleep, people tend to be more rigid in their thinking and less adaptable to new information. Poor sleep also causes deficits in attention. Fortunately, improving sleep can restore clear thinking and improve your attention,[7] likely because of improved prefrontal function. For example, one fMRI study looked at brain activity during thinking and found that people with insomnia had reduced activity in both the dorsomedial and ventrolateral prefrontal cortex.[8] The insomniacs were treated without medication, simply using many of the same recommendations in this chapter, and improved their sleep quality significantly, which restored their prefrontal activity to normal levels. So if you can improve your sleep, your thinking and decision-making abilities will improve too.

Reduce Prefrontal Worrying

Do you ever wake up in the middle of the night and have trouble falling back asleep? This is common in depression. These awakenings are caused by increased activity in the prefrontal cortex and anterior cingulate during slow-wave sleep, when the brain is supposed to be relaxed.[9] This increased activity is likely related to planning and worrying, which are known to cause sleep problems.[10] Anything you can do to reduce planning or worrying before bedtime will help the quality of your sleep.

Write down your worries. As we've discussed, worrying disrupts sleep because it activates the prefrontal cortex—and so does planning. If you're worrying or planning while trying to fall asleep, write down your thoughts. Get them out of your head and onto a piece of paper and be done with it.

Improve Frontal-Limbic Communication

Insomnia and depression are a two-way street—if you have insomnia, you're more likely to develop depression, and vice versa.[11] The connection between insomnia and depression probably has many causes, but one big culprit is communication between the prefrontal cortex and limbic system during sleep.

As I discussed in chapter 1, depression is a dysfunction in frontal-limbic communication, and you may remember that the hippocampus is an essential part of the limbic system. During sleep, the hippocampus talks to the prefrontal cortex by sending bursts of communication that the prefrontal cortex responds to.[12] Thus sleep is important for proper frontal-limbic communication, which is why disrupting your sleep can be so harmful, and why improving your sleep is such a great way to start an upward spiral.

Enhance Learning and Memory

The hippocampus, which is essential to forming new memories, functions properly only when you've had a full night's sleep.[13] Similarly, the dorsolateral prefrontal cortex's contribution to learning is also hobbled by poor sleep.

That means that quality sleep is essential for learning and memory. In particular, sleep selectively enhances memory for future-relevant information,[14] which helps you be more effective at achieving your goals. Furthermore, sleep enhances the learning for rewarding activities,[15] which means you'll have an easier time focusing on the positive.

And remember, it's quality, not just quantity. In one Dutch study, researchers used slight sound disturbances to keep people from staying in slow-wave sleep.[16] The subjects still spent the same amount of time sleeping, but they had lower-quality sleep, and thus experienced impaired functioning of the hippocampus.

Make your environment comfortable. Quality sleep requires calming the brain, while being uncomfortable activates the brain's stress response. If your bedroom is too cold or hot, too bright, noisy, or even smelly, your sleep could be disrupted without your conscious awareness. So do something about it. If there's noise you can't get rid of, add a white-noise maker like a fan, because that's less distracting to the brain.

The types of disruptions used in the Dutch study would be similar to sleeping in a slightly noisy room, like one with the television on low. This means that even though you may be getting enough sleep, you could probably still improve the quality of your sleep, which will enhance your frontal-limbic communication and improve your learning and memory.

Prepare Your Melatonin

When you have good sleep hygiene, your brain releases melatonin approximately thirty minutes before it's planning to go to sleep. That melatonin is produced from serotonin and helps prepare your brain for quality sleep. Melatonin release and sleep are both improved by exposure to sunlight.[17] So try getting more sun in the middle of the day.

Brighten your day. Bright lights during the day help synchronize your circadian rhythms and improve your sleep. So take a few minutes to go walking in the sunshine. This has the added benefit of boosting your serotonin[18] and reducing pain.[19] One study looked at patients recovering from spinal surgery in the hospital. Patients who were on the sunny side of the hospital had less stress and needed less pain medication. If you can't be near a window or go outside, at least try to work in a brightly lit environment while the sun is shining.

Increased sunlight exposure improves melatonin release and improves sleep.[20] So try getting more sun in the middle of the day.

Improve Your Mood with Serotonin

The Romantic poet William Wordsworth called sleep the "mother of fresh thoughts and joyous health." While lack of sleep worsens your mood and increases anxiety and stress,[21] improving the quality of your sleep has the reverse effect, likely because of the serotonin system. For example, increasing serotonin can increase slow-wave sleep and decrease REM sleep,[22] and it can even reduce the chances of waking up in the middle of the night.

In addition, serotonin activity both affects and is affected by circadian rhythms.[23] Interestingly, you have neurons that stretch from your eye to the brainstem region that produces serotonin, which are stimulated by ambient levels of light.[24] Another reason to make sure you get plenty of bright light during the day.

Circadian rhythms by themselves can impact your mood—they're the reason that positive emotions are generally lower in the morning and peak in early evening.[25] People can be affected by circadian rhythms differently, which explains why some people are night owls and others early birds. The effect of circadian rhythms on mood is important to understand, because sometimes when you feel crappy and think your life is falling apart, it's just your circadian rhythms slightly altering your mood. Yes, it's unfortunate that you don't have total control over it, but it can help if you accept this and realize that you'll need to create an upward spiral some other way or simply wait it out for a couple hours.

Reduce Your Stress with Norepinephrine

Sleep disruptions are a big source of stress. It's one of the reasons why new parents are so stressed, as well as new on-call doctors. In fact, people with insomnia have increased stress hormone levels before and during sleep.[26] That's really a bummer, because quality sleep helps prepare your brain to deal with stress. Chronically not getting enough sleep reduces the production of norepinephrine receptors in the whole frontal cortex,[27] and unfortunately, prefrontal norepinephrine is necessary for appropriately responding to stress. Reducing stress improves sleep, and improving sleep reduces stress—yet another upward spiral.

Reward Your Dopamine System with Quality Sleep

The dopamine system helps modulate both slow-wave sleep and REM sleep.[28] Furthermore, not only does dopamine have a large effect on sleep (as well as on pain and depression) but sleep, pain, and depression all also affect the dopamine system.[29] In addition, many aspects of the dopamine system are influenced by circadian rhythms,[30] including the production of dopamine receptors, dopamine transporters, and dopamine itself.

Reducing Pain with Endorphins

Your sleep, your mood, and your pain levels all interact.[31] Poor sleep can cause more negative moods and increased pain, which can lead to worse sleep.[32] In people with chronic pain, poor sleep quality increases pain, and this effect is even larger for people with depressed mood.[33] So poor sleep increases your pain and depresses your mood. And your depressed mood further worsens your pain, and both can then affect your sleep. That might sound like a big pain in the butt, but it also means that if you can change one part of the equation, you can affect all three.

Importantly, the biggest increase in pain comes from disrupting sleep throughout the night.[34] That means that the most important factor is not the total amount of sleep, but the amount of *continuous* sleep. So do what you can to sleep uninterrupted. This also suggests that taking naps as a regular substitute for sleep probably won't help with your pain.

The pain-reducing effects of quality sleep come from the brain's own type of morphine, *endorphins*. One recent study conducted at Johns Hopkins found that people with poor sleep quality have fewer endorphins in a wide variety of brain regions, including the dorsolateral prefrontal cortex and the anterior cingulate.[35] Sleep-related endorphin changes can explain why a good night's sleep is so beneficial to reducing pain.

Sleep Cleans the Brain

Your brain, through all its activity, generates trash in the form of broken-down chemicals. Just like the trash in your kitchen, it needs to be taken out, or it will start to pile up and get in your way. Sleep is important in clearing waste products that interfere with proper brain function.[36] Cleaning this harmful gunk out of the brain may be part of the reason that sleep feels so restorative.

Improve Your Sleep Hygiene

Studies show that knowledge about sleep hygiene improves sleep hygiene practices, which in turn improves sleep quality.[37] So just by reading this chapter, you're on the right track. And here are some more concrete tips to prepare your brain for a great night's sleep.

Sleep for eight hours straight. Most people need about eight hours of sleep. In general, the older you are, the less sleep you need. In college, you need about eight hours and twenty-four minutes. By the time you start drawing Social Security, you might need only seven. The important thing is to sleep in one continuous block (seven hours plus a one-hour nap is not the same). So don't take regular naps. And if you consistently get quality sleep, you won't even feel that you need them.

Use your bed/bedroom for sleeping. Don't do work in bed or in your bedroom. Don't surf the Internet. Don't watch television. If you use your bedroom only for sleeping, your brain associates your bed only with sleep, which will induce sleepiness like Pavlovian conditioning. Of course, it's also okay to have sex there (some might say more than okay).

Create a routine for preparing for sleep. Do it every night—a ritual to separate yourself from the rest of your hectic day. Your prefrontal cortex, in particular, needs to wind down, so if you're doing everything at sixty miles per hour and then plopping into bed, you may have difficulty falling asleep or getting quality sleep. A bedtime ritual might involve brushing your teeth, washing your face, going to the bathroom, then reading for a few minutes. Or you could include having a cup of herbal tea, or reading to your kids, or saying your prayers—any relaxing activity. Meditation can also be helpful. Again, sex is okay, but probably can't be relied upon as part of your regular routine (if it can, props to you).

Avoid caffeine near bedtime. Duh. Even if you can fall asleep while caffeinated, caffeine disrupts proper sleep architecture and reduces sleep quality. So no black tea, green tea, coffee, or Red Bull within a few hours of sleep.

Eat and drink in moderation. Don't eat a large meal less than three hours before bedtime. Indigestion can interfere with sleep, and acid reflux is more common once you're horizontal. However, a small snack of simple food is okay, and it's even helpful if hunger is a distraction. Similarly, thirst can disrupt sleep, so have a couple sips of water before bed. But don't chug a whole glass, or your bladder will wake you up in the middle of the night.

Don't use alcohol as a regular sleep aid. A beer or a glass of wine can help you fall asleep faster, but it disrupts your sleep architecture, so your night's not as restful.[38] On top of that, the more often you use alcohol to fall asleep, the less it works. Lastly, alcohol abuse can lead to the same types of reduced slow-wave sleep and increased REM sleep that is seen in depression.[39]

Exercise. Make physical activity a regular part of your life. Exercise improves sleep by synchronizing circadian rhythms, reducing stress, decreasing REM sleep, and inducing numerous neurochemical changes.[40] Exercising too close to bedtime, however, may make it difficult to fall asleep, so try to do it a few hours before.

Try Cognitive Behavioral Therapy

Cognitive behavioral therapy for insomnia (CBT-I) includes good sleep hygiene but also addresses potentially maladaptive thoughts and habits that disrupt your sleep. CBT-I improves alertness, thinking, and sleep quality better than sleep hygiene alone does,[41] and it can be an effective treatment for depression.[42] A professional therapist can help you take the most advantage of CBT-I, but here are a few simple CBT-I tips.

Keep a sleep diary. If you see a sleep professional, the first thing she'll ask you to do is keep a sleep diary. The simplest sleep diary involves writing down the time you went to bed and woke up, but including more info can make it even more useful. Try writing down the time you intended to wake up and go to sleep, how long you thought it took you to fall asleep, your stress levels, any medications you took or what you ate, what activities you did before you went to bed, and the quality of your sleep. There are also many online resources available to help you keep a sleep diary. After a week, see if you notice any patterns in what helps you sleep better and what makes you sleep worse. Even if keeping a sleep diary on your own doesn't seem to help, if nothing else, you can bring your sleep diary to a sleep professional, and this will help you get a jump on the solution.

Reduce anxiety. Are you anxious about getting enough sleep? Recognizing this can reduce excess limbic activity. Use the tips in chapter 2 to help.

Restrict your sleep. The hardest part of insomnia is lying there, unable to fall asleep. Sometimes the solution is to stop trying. If you always try to sleep for eight hours but only ever get six, try just sleeping for six. If you usually go to bed at eleven but can't fall asleep till midnight, then go to sleep at midnight—but wake up at the same time. Once you start having more continuous sleep and are spending less time tossing and turning, then you can gradually change your bedtime.

Just chill. The more you move around, the harder it is to fall asleep, so pick a comfortable position and lie there. Don't look at the clock; don't adjust your pillow; just relax. If you can't stay calm, get out of bed and go to another room. Do something relaxing for twenty or thirty minutes, then try again.

Chapter 8

Develop Positive Habits

In the spring of 1870, a young William James was suffering from a "crisis of meaning," full of anxiety and melancholy. But after reading an essay on free will, he realized that he could change his mood by changing his habits. Within three years, he began teaching at Harvard and ultimately became the father of American psychology. In 1890 he wrote, "The great thing, then, in all education, is to make our nervous system our ally instead of our enemy... We must make automatic and habitual, as early as possible, as many useful actions as we can." Even then he understood the power of life changes to cause brain changes, although now we have the neuroscience to back it up.

Habits are the things you do when you're not thinking about what to do. In chapter 4, I talked about how your brain gets stuck in bad habits—how the dorsal striatum controls routines and the nucleus accumbens controls impulses. In this chapter, we'll discuss how to get those same brain regions working for you instead of against you. This will allow you to take advantage of the brain's habit system to get things done, so you won't always have to rely entirely on your overworked prefrontal cortex. Developing good habits can be a powerful boost to an upward spiral, because once you set those habits in motion, you can start to change your life without any additional effort.

How We Create Habits

We've already discussed how habits are created by repetition. But let's say it again. Habits are created by repetition. Interestingly, some habits require less repetition than others, because some actions inherently release more dopamine. Unfortunately, bad habits are the ones that often release lots of dopamine, so you don't need to do them very often to get hooked. Smoking releases a lot of dopamine in the nucleus accumbens, so you don't have to smoke very many cigarettes to start a habit. In contrast, flossing doesn't release very much dopamine, so you have to floss every day for a long time to make it a habit.

Of course, when you first try to create a new habit, it requires an effort. You won't always feel like going to the gym or staying calm or calling up a friend. That's because the right connections within the striatum have not yet been established and strengthened. Starting a new habit requires intervention by the prefrontal cortex, and that takes mental effort. It takes even more mental effort in depression.

The good news is that the dorsal striatum responds to repetition. It doesn't matter if you want to do something—every single time you do it, it gets further wired into the dorsal striatum. The first few times will be the most difficult, because they will rely on the prefrontal cortex. But if you can power through, things will feel easier as the burden of action shifts from the consciously effortful prefrontal cortex to the unconsciously effortless dorsal striatum.

Self-Affirmation Helps Change Your Habits

Two studies from the United Kingdom figured out a clever way to help change your bad habits. The trick is self-affirmation, which may sound hokey, but the results were undeniable. The first study had smokers answer a set of questions.[1] Members of the control group were asked somewhat random questions about their opinions, such as "Is chocolate the best flavor of ice cream?" But those in the "self-affirmation" group were asked questions that made them focus on the best parts of themselves: "Have you ever forgiven another person when they have hurt you?" or "Have you ever been considerate of another person's feelings?" If the participants answered yes, they were asked to elaborate, which drew their attention to their positive qualities. Then both groups read an informational packet on the negative health effects of smoking.

The study found that smokers in the self-affirmation group developed a greater intention to quit smoking and also were more likely to start looking into how to quit. Importantly, the effect of self-affirmation was strongest on the heaviest smokers. That means for the people who are the worst off, a little self-affirmation does the most good.

A second study was organized in a similar way, except that participants received information about the benefits of healthier eating. The study found the self-affirmation group ate significantly more fruits and vegetables over the next week.[2]

Self-affirmation. Before thinking about which habits you'd like to change, answer this list of questions with a yes or a no. If you answer yes to any questions, please elaborate.

1. Have you ever forgiven another person when he or she has hurt you?

2. Have you ever been considerate of another person's feelings?

3. Have you ever given money or items to someone less fortunate than you?

4. Have you ever tried to cheer someone up who had had a bad day?

5. Have you ever encouraged a friend to pursue a goal?

These studies show that thinking about your positive qualities makes it easier to change your habits. That's a cool phenomenon, but what's the neuroscience behind it?

We know from other studies that happy memories boost serotonin.[3] Positive self-reflection likely has the same effect on increasing serotonin activity. This is important, because serotonin is essential for proper functioning of the prefrontal cortex. In addition, self-reflection and intentional regulation of emotions activate the medial prefrontal cortex.[4] Thus self-affirmation helps the thinking prefrontal cortex override the habitual striatum to great results.

Reducing Your Stress

Medical residents have to deal with long hours, late nights, difficult patients, and the fear that they'll make a mistake and accidentally kill someone. In short, they're stressed. On top of that, in order to become full-fledged doctors, they have to spend months studying intensely to pass their board-certifying exam. In short, they're extra-stressed.

To study the effects of chronic stress, researchers in Portugal performed fMRI scans on a stressed group of residents who had just spent three months studying for their board exam and compared them to a control group of residents who had no exam.[5] The study found that stressed subjects acted more out of habit than intention. They kept making the same choices, even when those choices were rewarded less and less. Not surprisingly, the increased habitual behavior was caused by changes in processing within the habitual dorsal striatum. In addition, the stress caused the decision-making orbitofrontal cortex to actually shrink. The subjects were studied again six weeks later, after they'd gotten a chance to relax—and indeed, their dorsal striatum activity had returned to normal, as had the size of their orbitofrontal cortices.

Stress biases the brain toward old habits over intentional actions, which is one of the reasons it is so hard to change coping habits—the things we do to deal with stress. One of the problems with coping habits is that if you don't do them, you stay stressed. And if you try to suppress a coping habit, you're more stressed, which makes your brain want to do that coping habit even more. Clearly this is a downward spiral, and the best solution is to find other ways to reduce your stress.

Reducing your stress levels can be accomplished through many means: exercise (chapter 5), decision making (chapter 6), improving sleep hygiene (chapter 7), biofeedback (chapter 9), gratitude (chapter 10), and social interactions (chapter 11). Even if you can't reduce your stress as much as you'd like to, a little stress has some benefits: habits are learned more deeply when you're stressed.[6] So if you can manage to change your habits, even a little bit, your efforts will have a more powerful effect than trying to change your habits when not stressed.

Accept That You Won't Be Perfect

In a commencement address in 2012, author and graphic novelist Neil Gaiman made the keen observation that "if you're making mistakes, it means you're out there doing something." Changing habits does not require that you make zero mistakes; in fact, mistakes are almost inevitable. As I said above, habits are created by repetition, that is, by *practice*. You continually practice your habits, the same way LeBron James continually practices his jump shot. Because it's practice, it makes sense that you'll make mistakes—lots of mistakes, particularly in the beginning.

Old habits persist because of striatum activity. Fortunately, when you want to create a new good habit, like going to the gym or eating healthier foods or even just taking a shower to start your day, the prefrontal cortex can override the striatum. The problem is that the prefrontal cortex can only override it insofar as it's paying attention, and it's impossible for your prefrontal cortex to be eternally vigilant. It has a lot to do and only so many resources for paying attention. When you stop paying attention because of distraction or stress, the striatum takes over, and you don't realize it until you're halfway through that pint of Cherry Garcia.

Resolve to change. Making a resolution to change is more effective than simply wanting to change, and dramatically increases your chance of success.[7] Being specific in what you want to change helps make it more achievable. For example, "I resolve to work out more" is not as effective as "I resolve to go to the gym before work on Tuesdays and Thursdays."

Think of your striatum as a dog that needs to be trained. If you leave a plate of cookies sitting out on the coffee table and the dog eats them, you can't really get mad at the dog. That's what dogs do. What did you expect? If you were standing there, staring at your dog the whole time, maybe the cookies would be safe, but eventually your phone would ring or you'd have to go to work. It's the same with your brain. If you haven't trained your striatum to stop eating cookies, what exactly are you expecting will happen when your prefrontal cortex stops watching?

Often when we try to start a good habit and then slip up, we describe it as a failure of willpower. But sticking to a good habit is not simply a matter of willpower. You have willpower only insofar as your prefrontal cortex is paying attention and has enough serotonin to work properly. Yes, deciding that you want to do things differently is an important first step, but your striatum doesn't care that much about what you want; it cares about repetition.

You won't succeed 100 percent of the time—or maybe even most of the time—but getting upset with yourself does not help the process of retraining the brain. It hinders it. Those feelings of frustration or self-judgment are all sources of stress, making it more likely that you'll keep doing your old habits. The key to change comes in the moment after you realize you didn't enact your intended habit. That special moment is an opportunity for the prefrontal cortex to reassert itself, to remind yourself of your goal and try again. Yes, you will probably have many slipups, but if you give up after a slipup, you've only trained your striatum to give up. You'll probably hear a little voice inside your head telling you to give up, but the more you listen to that voice, the more it becomes habit and the harder it is to resist. Every time you stick to your goals, the voice gets softer.

Be as patient and kind with yourself as you would be with a cute little puppy that you're trying to house-train. Stressing the puppy out will only make it pee on the floor. When your habit doesn't take at first, just go for it again. And again…and again—and eventually it'll start to stick.

Increasing Serotonin for Better Habits

Imagine there's a marshmallow sitting on a plate in front of you. A nice lady in a lab coat sits next to you. She says she's going to leave the room, and you can eat the marshmallow if you want. But if you wait for her to get back, she'll give you *two* marshmallows. Oh and by the way, you're only four years old in this scenario. So which is it: one marshmallow now or two later? Choose wisely. It may impact the rest of your life.

This famous experiment was conducted over forty years ago. Kids who waited to get the second marshmallow grew up to be more successful than kids who ate the one in front of them right away. They had higher SAT scores, were more likely to go to college, and were less likely to use drugs.[8] The marshmallow experiment is really a test of your prefrontal cortex's serotonin function and its ability to override the habitual and impulsive striatum. In fact, when the kids from the original marshmallow experiment were scanned in an fMRI forty years later, they even had differences in prefrontal activity.[9] The ones who had waited for the marshmallow as four-year-olds had greater ventrolateral prefrontal activity, which, unsurprisingly, helps control impulses.

Luckily, your serotonin system is not set in stone at four years old. It's possible to enhance serotonin activity, making it easier to create good habits[10]—and here are a few ways to do so.

Sunlight

When humans first began evolving, there were fewer LED screens and fluorescent-lit cubicles, and people got their light from the sun. Sunlight holds distinct advantages over artificial light. First, the ultraviolet (UV) rays in sunlight, when absorbed through the skin, allow your body to produce vitamin D, which has many important functions, including promoting serotonin production. Second, sunlight is a lot more intense than most artificial light. You may think the lights in your office are bright, but that's just because your eyes are good at adjusting to ambient light. In reality, the intensity of light on a bright, sunny day is about one hundred times higher. Bright sunlight improves serotonin production and keeps the serotonin transporter from sucking it away (which is also one thing that antidepressants do). Lastly, the scattered sunlight that creates the blue of the sky is the ideal color to stimulate the photoreceptors that control your circadian rhythms. So it's better at promoting quality sleep than artificial light.

Massage

Numerous studies have examined the effects of massage on everyone from babies and new mothers to breast-cancer survivors and people who suffer from migraines. The results are fairly clear that massage boosts your serotonin by as much as 30 percent.[11] Massage also decreases stress hormones and raises dopamine levels, which helps you create new good habits.

Exercise

We discussed this extensively in chapter 5, but it bears repeating: exercise increases both serotonin production and release. In particular, aerobic exercises, like running and biking, are best at boosting serotonin. Interestingly, if you try to do too much exercise or feel forced to do it, it may not have the right effect. Recognizing that you are choosing to exercise changes its neurochemical effect. That may be a result of your ancient instincts—the difference between running because you're hunting something and running because it's hunting you.

Remembering Happy Memories

This may seem like the hokiest piece of the puzzle, but it may be the most important. It's also the simplest to do. All you need to do is remember positive events that have happened in your life. This simple act increases serotonin production in the anterior cingulate cortex.[12] The same study also showed that remembering sad events decreased serotonin production in the anterior cingulate. Thus, remembering positive events has a twofold effect: it increases serotonin and also keeps you from thinking about negative events.

Remember the good times. Maybe you can remember a special birthday from childhood or a fun trip or even something as simple as a pleasant Sunday afternoon. Try to visualize it in detail or, better yet, write it down for future reference. If you're having difficulty, talk to an old friend, look at photographs, or read your diary from happier times. Repeat as necessary.

Activate Your Prefrontal Cortex

In depression, goal-directed, intentional actions are not in balance with habits and impulses, because the prefrontal cortex is not appropriately controlling the striatum. To start creating good habits, you need to activate the prefrontal cortex in the right way.

Keep Long-Term Goals in Mind

The German philosopher Friedrich Nietzsche wrote, "He who has a *why* to live for can bear almost any *how*." Having long-term goals gives you a *why*.

To accomplish something really important to you, it's necessary to suppress a lot of short-term impulses. If you want to get good grades in college, you have to skip a lot of parties; if you want to be an attentive parent, you have to watch less television. That means you're missing out on the dopamine release that accompanies those impulses. Fortunately, suppressing an impulse doesn't always have to decrease your dopamine—it can actually feel good. The key is the prefrontal cortex, which is responsible for pursuing long-term goals and has the ability to modulate dopamine release in the nucleus accumbens.[13] So suppressing an impulse can be rewarding, as long as it's in service of your larger values. For example, it can be satisfying to stay home and study instead of going to a movie if your dream is to become a doctor. Or it can be rewarding to suppress that impulse to shop till you drop if you're saving the money for your kid's college fund.

Think about how your life would improve. How would your life be better if your bad habit was gone? In a study on alcoholics, subjects were asked to use this type of thinking while looking at pictures of alcohol. Focusing on how life would be better reduced activity in the dorsal striatum and nucleus accumbens.[14] Reducing alcohol-related routines and impulses prepared them to change their drinking habits.

If you don't have any long-term goals, that can explain why it's hard to develop good habits. If you need help developing long-term goals, refer back to chapter 6. And when an impulse arises, try consciously reminding yourself of your values and goals. That will help activate the prefrontal cortex in the right way and make your short-term sacrifices more rewarding.

Have Some Self-Awareness

Self-awareness is a mindfulness technique that helps activate the prefrontal cortex. It simply means that you should try to become consciously aware of your emotions and your emotional response to other people and the outside world. Emotional awareness increases activity in the ventrolateral prefrontal cortex, which then communicates through the medial prefrontal cortex to reduce amygdala reactivity.[15] That means that if you can have the wherewithal to recognize your feelings when you're upset, sad, anxious, or stressed, you'll actually feel a little better.

Change Your Environment

Once habits are stored in your striatum, they are triggered by a thought, a feeling, or something in your environment. Thoughts and feelings are not always controllable, but your environment often is.

As we discussed in chapter 4, we often get stuck in habits because our environment keeps triggering them. Ideally, then, we should identify the specific environmental cue that's triggering the habit (for more insight, see Charles Duhigg's *The Power of Habit*) and just avoid or change that cue. If you always come home from the grocery store with cookies, next time don't even let yourself walk down the cookie aisle.

If you can't determine a specific trigger, try randomly changing anything you don't like about your environment. Maybe just hang a different picture in the living room, or paint your bedroom, or even move to a new apartment. Start a new job. Go on vacation. Get a new hobby. Buy some new clothes. This may sound like strange advice, but the limbic system is very good at picking up subtle environmental cues, and because it has a lot of connections with the striatum, even subtle changes can have a big effect.

Of course, part of the problem is that no matter where you go, you are bringing your own tendencies with you. But changing yourself is often easiest when you change your environment first.

Productive Procrastination

Maybe you want to go to the gym, or you have a project due at work or some chore to do around the house. Despite the fact that the deadline is approaching, you just can't work up the energy or motivation. And the more you procrastinate, the more anxiety you feel. Trying to force yourself to do a project when you have no energy or motivation is akin to sitting in your car and trying to change directions without first stepping on the gas. Sure you can sit there and turn the wheel, but nothing happens. The key is to start driving.

The same can be true of things you need to do. Procrastinating by checking Facebook or watching terrible reality-television shows—or by even doing nothing at all—is like sitting in your car playing with the steering wheel. It won't get you anywhere. Instead, just start doing something productive—anything productive—even if it's not the thing you're supposed to be doing. Wash one dish in the sink. Put on your shoes. Send one work email. Do anything that's on your to-do list that needs to be checked off, even if it's not anywhere near the top. It still needs to get done, and it keeps you moving forward.

Once you start being productive, dopamine is released in the striatum and parts of the prefrontal cortex. Suddenly you'll have more energy and motivation to do the thing you really need to do. It's perfectly fine to procrastinate a little; just try being more productive in your procrastination.

Like William James, you can make your nervous system an ally instead of an enemy. You have the power to create good habits, and good habits have the power to reverse the course of depression.

Chapter 9

Take Advantage of Biofeedback

My dad is a pretty happy and relaxed guy, and some of that comes from the three times a week he drives to a dance studio tucked above a RadioShack. In the bright, hardwood-floored room, a muscular man with a shaved head and surfing shorts whispers instructions in a mix of English and Sanskrit. My dad and the rest of the class bend and twist into strange shapes, the windows fogging over with the moisture of their collective breath.

My dad has been doing yoga for almost ten years. I've always loved sports, but for years I didn't get what was so great about this odd form of extended stretching. But after starting yoga myself—and learning more about the neuroscience of depression—this ancient practice began to reshape my understanding of the relationship between the body and the brain.

For decades, yogis have claimed that yoga can improve depression, decrease chronic pain, and reduce stress—and even improve the immune system and lower blood pressure. This may sound like a lot of new age foolishness, but surprisingly, everything in that list has now been supported by scientific research. It seems a bit magical that posing like a proud warrior or a crow could have such extensive effects, but it's not magic; it's neuroscience.

This chapter is not just about yoga. It's about *biofeedback*, which is simply the fact that the brain changes its activity based on what the body is doing. It just so happens that yoga enhances brain changes through conscious biofeedback. People sometimes think biofeedback requires technology, like a heart-rate monitor or some device that tells you what your body is doing. And while technology can make it easier for *you* to understand body changes, your brain doesn't need it. It is perfectly capable of paying attention to your body—your heart rate, your breathing rate, your muscle tension, and dozens of other bodily activities. In fact, your brain is paying attention to all those things all the time, whether or not you're conscious of it.

Try yoga. Yoga utilizes almost every suggestion in this chapter, including stretching, breathing, relaxation, and posture changes, and it can, in fact, help treat depression.[1] Yoga poses that incorporate back bends and opening the chest do a particularly good job at increasing positive emotions.

We know our brains can control our bodies, particularly when it comes to things like emotions. When you feel scared or excited, your heart beats faster; when you feel frustrated, you clench your jaw. But it turns out, like almost everything else in this book, emotions aren't a one-way street. They're a feedback loop. The brain changes its activity based on what the body is doing.

Even actions as simple as changing your posture, relaxing your face, or slowing your breathing can have dramatic effects on your brain activity and, subsequently, your stress, your thoughts, and your mood. These changes are often transient, but they can be long lasting, particularly if they entail changing a habit. You can further improve the biofeedback by increasing your awareness of your body.

How Biofeedback Works

Your brain constantly receives signals from the rest of the body telling it how to feel. Learning to understand and control these signals is a big part of kick-starting an upward spiral.

You have several brain regions devoted to sensations from your body. Each of your senses (taste, smell, hearing, touch, and sight) has its own patch of *sensory cortex*. Additionally, some sensations also have emotional components that are further processed by the insula. The different types of sensory processing are most evident when it comes to pain. For example, if you hit your forehead on the kitchen cabinet, the touch cortex might notice it, thinking, *Something just bumped against my head*, whereas the insula would process, *Ouch! Ow, ow, ow!*

Are you hungry or stressed? Unfortunately, emotional sensations are not very precise, and your brain often misinterprets them. For example, your brain receives a signal that something is happening in your stomach. It may interpret it as hunger, but in fact, it might just be that you're stressed, or vice versa. These types of signals are like your car's check-engine light—alerting you that something is happening, but not being very helpful in telling you what. Calmly doing a self-assessment of your feelings can help distinguish the signals.

In addition to pain, many other sensations have emotional components, such as tense muscles or a queasy stomach. The neural signals for these sensations are carried by the *vagus nerve*, which runs throughout your upper body and sends information to your brain about your heart rate, breathing, digestion, and other bodily functions that usually have an emotional component.

Biofeedback in Depression

Remember how your mom would say, "Stop making that face, or it'll stay that way?" She was kinda right. Frowning makes you feel worse and thus more likely to frown. If you're not aware of the power of biofeedback, it can unintentionally lead you into or keep you in a downward spiral.

In depression, people tend to inadvertently generate many negative types of biofeedback—for instance, a timid or withdrawn posture, usually accompanied by shoulders slouched down and forward, increases their feelings of sadness. People with depression also suffer from increased muscle tension, which heightens feelings of anxiety,[2] and reduced *heart-rate variability,*[3] which has a big impact on your mood—whether you've heard of it or not.

Heart-rate variability is exactly what it sounds like: most healthy people's heart rates jump around a little bit—a little faster here, a little slower there. Information travels by the vagus nerve and causes your heart rate to slow down every time you exhale. However, people with depression have less activity in the vagus nerve, so the heart does not change speed as much. Their heartbeats remain steady, like a metronome. This is important enough that electrical stimulation of the vagus nerve is actually a treatment for depression (chapter 12). Unfortunately, direct stimulation of the vagus nerve requires surgery, but it's possible to stimulate it yourself through your own actions, which we'll discuss below.

A splash of cold water. Sudden cold water on your face slows down your heart rate by indirectly stimulating the vagus nerve. If you're feeling overwhelmed, stressed, or anxious, find a sink, fill your hands with cold water, and splash it on your face.

Negative facial expression, withdrawn posture, increased muscle tension, and reduced heart-rate variability are all symptoms of being depressed. However, as is the case with so many aspects of our brains, these are not just results of depression, but also part of the cause.

Use the power of music. Whether playing an instrument or listening to the radio, music increases heart-rate variability, though making music has a stronger effect.[4] Music engages most of the limbic system, including the hippocampus, anterior cingulate, and nucleus accumbens, which is why it can be motivating and enjoyable and can help regulate your emotions.[5] It can also be soothing, lowering blood pressure[6] and reducing stress. So sing along with the radio or just make a playlist of your favorite songs. Better yet, go dancing. Dancing combines music, exercise, and being social, so you get a triple boost to an upward spiral.

The good news is that you can change the feedback. If the brain gets signals from the body that it should feel calm (for example, you're taking long, slow breaths) or happy (you're smiling and holding your head high), then it's more likely to feel calm and happy. Here's how.

Smile

Your smile is a powerful tool. Most people think that we smile because we feel happy, but it can go the other way as well: we feel happy because we smile.

Smiling increases positive feelings. One classic study from the 1980s tricked people into inadvertently smiling or frowning by using a pencil.[7] Participants were not told that the experiment was meant to study emotion but instead were asked to hold a pencil in one of three ways: between their teeth without their lips touching it, between their lips, or in their hand. Holding a pencil between your teeth without letting your lips touch it forces the mouth into a kind of smile. Holding it between your lips makes it impossible to smile and forces you to make a kind of frown. The pencil-in-hand group was the control group. Once situated, the participants looked at cartoons and rated how funny they were. The "smile" group found the cartoons much funnier than the "frown" group, while the control group was somewhere in the middle.

Smile. It's simple and improves your mood; you don't even need a pencil. Don't do it for others or in the mirror. Just relax the tension in your face and let the corners of your mouth drift up. The complex and amazing process of biofeedback will jump into action.

In a more recent study, participants viewed a series of emotional faces and were instructed to either raise their cheeks (that is, smile) or contract their eyebrows (that is, frown).[8] When participants were smiling, they found the facial expressions in the pictures more pleasant than when they were frowning. So when you smile, you're more likely to perceive positive emotions in other people, which can have a big influence on your mood. On top of that, the effects of even a brief smile persisted for several minutes.

> **Laugh.** If you want to get the biggest facial feedback benefit, laugh. Even if nothing is funny, just open your mouth and let out a "ha-ha-ha." The brain doesn't distinguish much between genuine laughter and fake laughter,[9] and fake laughing can often lead to laughing at yourself for real.

Facial feedback works because the brain senses the flexing of certain facial muscles (like the *zygomatic major* muscle at the corners of your mouth), to which the brain thinks, *I must be happy about something.* Similarly, if that muscle isn't flexed, your brain thinks, *Oh...I must not be happy.*

In addition to the direct neural feedback, in the real world, you also get the added advantage of social feedback. Smiles are infectious. So even if you don't feel much happier, the people around you are more likely to smile, and that can improve your mood as well.

Lastly, if you can work up the energy to genuinely smile, you'll probably have an even bigger benefit. This is also a great tip for becoming more photogenic. While the zygomatic major controls the corners of your mouth and can be used to make fake smiles, a muscle at the corner of the eyes—the *orbicularis oculi*—flexes only when you're actually smiling. The reason many people think their smiles look fake in pictures is that those smiles *are* fake—the corners of their eyes are not flexed.

Stand Up Straight

Your mother was right again: stop slouching. If you want to be confident and decisive, then stand up straight and open your chest to the world. Your posture is an important source of biofeedback. One German study had participants make decisions while standing in either a confident or doubtful posture.[10] When people stood in a confident posture, they were more decisive. So if you want to be more decisive, take a decisive stance (literally).

A confident posture also makes you more confident in your own thoughts and beliefs in general. One Spanish study sat participants in a confident or doubtful posture while writing about their own positive or negative qualities.[11] Subjects in the confident posture believed more strongly in what they wrote, whether it was good or bad. Confidence in their positive qualities made them more optimistic.

In addition, a confident posture enhances the effect of compliments from other people. In a study from Texas, researchers placed participants in either a confident or doubtful posture and told them they were good at taking tests.[12] When later given a difficult test, doubtful posture subjects gave up more easily, while confident posture subjects tried harder. Remember, they were all complimented on their test-taking abilities, but the confident posture subjects internalized this positive information.

A confident posture may not automatically make you happier, but it does modulate your brain's response to your thoughts. So if you want to be more confident (for example, *I'm going to ace this job interview*, or *I'm going to quit smoking*), think positive thoughts while sticking your chest out and keeping your chin up. Similarly, if someone compliments you, act like you believe it.

On top of your own brain's response, posture can also have a social feedback component. It's easy to think of your mood as being completely determined by yourself, but other people will automatically perceive and react to your posture. You will (consciously or unconsciously) notice their reactions and be affected by them. A confident posture makes people more confident in you. So not only does your brain think, *Oh, I'm standing up straight, I must be confident*, it also thinks, *Wow, everyone seems to have a lot of confidence in me. I must be pretty confident.*

Lastly, beyond any effect on confidence, standing up straight can also increase your energy. One study in the journal *Biofeedback* showed that slouching decreases your energy levels,[13] and that this more strongly impacts people with higher levels of depression. People who have a tendency to feel bad feel even worse when they slouch. That means improvements in posture will have the biggest effect on people with the worst depression. Interestingly, the study also found that skipping increased energy levels (so maybe skip down the hall when no one's watching).

Changes in posture are reflected by changes in neurohormone levels. One study from Harvard found that standing or sitting in an open, expansive posture increases testosterone and decreases the stress hormone cortisol.[14] These changes in neurohormones likely contribute to the other effects of confident postures described above.

The take-home message is that if you're feeling doubtful, keep your chin up, stand up straight, and stick out your chest. It will help you be more decisive and internalize positive thoughts, and it will give you more energy.

Calm Your Face

Think about the middle of your forehead, just above the center of your eyebrows. Is there tension there? Are you concerned about something? This muscle is the *corrugator supercilii*, and it pulls your eyebrows down and together, causing your forehead to wrinkle (in other words, it gets its name from the fact that it makes your skin corrugated). It helps express displeasure, anger, worry, and other negative emotions. But your furrowed brow is also a cause of consternation and discontent. In the same way that your brain thinks you're happy when it senses that your "smile" muscles are flexed, your brain notices when your corrugator supercilii is flexed and thinks you're upset or worried.

Wear sunglasses. On bright days, we often contract our corrugator supercilii while squinting to reduce glare from the sun. So while it might be a beautiful day, you're sending signals to your brain that you're slightly upset. Sunglasses reduce glare so you don't have to squint. So they not only make you look cool, but also, thanks to facial feedback, they help you feel calmer.

In one clever study, participants had golf tees taped to each eyebrow and were asked to try to touch them together, which they could do only by furrowing their eyebrows.[15] When viewing pictures with their brows furrowed, they experienced more sadness. Brow furrowing also increases feelings of anger and disgust, and it makes people less happy, less agreeable, and less interested.[16]

Relax your jaw. Often, when stressed, we inadvertently clench our teeth, which increases overall tension. So let your jaw hang loose, wiggle it around, and then open wide. This may make you yawn, which will also increase your calmness.

So if your eyebrow muscles are tensed, you feel more negative emotions and fewer positive ones. What happens when they relax? Some interesting evidence comes from people with a little too much money who want to look a few years younger. I'm talking about botox. Botox is a neurotoxin that removes wrinkles by paralyzing certain facial muscles. Paralyzing the corrugator supercilli makes it very difficult to create a furrowed brow, and people who have had that treatment often experience less anxiety simply because they can't create the corresponding facial expression.[17] Unfortunately, they sometimes feel less joy as well, as they can't always fully express excitement or surprise.

It is very difficult to achieve inner peace when flexing the corrugator supercilii. A furrowed brow is a large part of what it means to feel—and create—negative emotions. When you start to feel anxious or stressed or angry, notice if your brow is furrowed. Try relaxing your forehead, and it should help diminish the feeling.

Change Your Breathing

Breathing is your most important bodily function, and like all basic functions (eating, sex, etc.), it is closely tied to the limbic system. People with breathing problems have a much higher risk of developing depression.[18] Changing your breathing is a powerful tool for creating an upward spiral, because it is one of the quickest ways to change your emotional state.

> **Take a deep breath.** When anxious or overwhelmed, slow breathing can help. Breathe in slowly through your nose while counting slowly to six (or even eight). Pause for a couple seconds at the top of your inhalation and then exhale slowly through your nose for the same count.

Different types of breathing have different effects on the body and the brain. A study from Sweden showed that a combination of different breathing types (slow, fast, and superfast) increases feelings of optimism and decreases feelings of depression, anxiety, and overall stress.[19]

Breathing affects the brain through signals carried by the vagus nerve. Not only does the vagus nerve send signals down to the heart, as mentioned earlier, but it also carries signals up into the brain stem. Vagus nerve signaling is important in activating circuits for resting and relaxation, known as the parasympathetic nervous system. The parasympathetic system is the opposite of the sympathetic nervous system, which controls the fight-or-flight instinct. Slow breathing increases activity in the vagus nerve and pushes the brain toward parasympathetic activity. So slow, deep breathing calms you down.

By contrast, rapid breathing deactivates the parasympathetic nervous system and activates the sympathetic nervous system. When you are anxious, excited, or scared, you breathe quickly. But it's also true that if you breathe quickly, you're more likely to feel those feelings. Fast breathing can make you more nervous—but also more excited. Sometimes that's a good thing. Maybe you need a bit more energy to make it to the gym (or to do anything at all).

Breathe faster for energy. Sometimes you feel that you need more energy. Try quick, shallow breaths for twenty to thirty seconds. Don't do it for too long, however, or you may start to feel light-headed.

Relax Your Muscles

When you're feeling stressed or anxious, your muscles tend to tense up, though you may not be consciously aware of it. Unfortunately, your brain senses the tension in your muscles and thinks, *I must be tense.* The interesting thing about muscles is that they don't flex on their own. When they're tight, it's because the brain is telling them to be tight. So how can you help your brain relax?

Clench and relax. To remind your brain to relax your muscles, sometimes it's helpful to clench them first. Take a deep breath in and then flex a tight muscle for a few seconds. After holding for a few seconds, exhale with a sigh and relax. The most important muscles to relax are your facial muscles, since those have the largest effect on emotion, but relaxing your hands, butt, and stomach are also important.

Stretching helps relax your muscles and goes a long way toward calming the nervous system. It is also stimulates endorphins and endocannabinoids,[20] which reduce pain. You don't need complex poses; any stretching will do.

Getting a massage is also a great way to relax your muscles. Massage reduces pain, stress, and anxiety, and it improves sleep.[21] The wide-ranging effects likely result from the fact that massage boosts your serotonin and dopamine levels and decreases cortisol.[22] Sometimes it's even helpful to give yourself a massage with a tennis ball by lying on it, leaning against it, or rolling it firmly against your muscles. It probably doesn't have all the same effects as getting a massage from a person, but it's cheap and quick, and it can still feel great.

But for now, just sit up straight and take a deep breath. Allow your face to relax and the corners of your mouth to drift up, and let biofeedback works its magic.

Chapter 10

Activate a Gratitude Circuit

In the late 1940s, the writer Albert Camus, suffering a bout of tuberculosis, journeyed from war-ravaged Paris to seek warmth and solace in his birthplace of northern Algeria. In a gray, rainy December, he found everything had changed and bitterly recognized the folly of hoping to relive his younger days. And yet he realized that the warm joy of his youth lay still untouched in his memory, writing, "In the depths of winter, I finally learned that within me is an invincible summer."

In depression, life is full of disappointments and lacking in things you sorely need—a good night's sleep, a job well done, a friendly face. While the gap between what you want and what you have may seem large, it is never as wide as it appears when you're weighed down by depression. As discussed in chapter 3, some brains are wired to focus more on the negative, and that tendency gets even worse in depression. But there is a powerful force that directly combats negativity, and it's called "gratitude."

Gratitude is a potent antidote to negativity, because it doesn't depend on your life circumstances. You could be poor and starving and yet still grateful for a warm breeze. Conversely, you could be rich and powerful and still be annoyed at the sound your husband makes when he's chewing. Gratitude is a state of mind—in fact, there's a gratitude circuit in your brain, badly in need of a workout. Strengthening that circuit brings the power to elevate your physical and mental health, boost happiness, improve sleep, and help you feel more connected to other people.

Benefits of Gratitude

Dozens of studies in recent years have shown the benefits of gratitude. Perhaps most importantly, gratitude improves mood.[1] When you think about and express more gratitude, it's easier to feel positive emotions.

Decreased Depression Symptoms

One of the biggest problems with depression is not simply the thought that life isn't worth living, but the possibility that you might act on that thought. It turns out that gratitude actually reduces the likelihood of suicidal thoughts.[2] Importantly, the effect of gratitude is greatest in people with the highest levels of hopelessness. When everything appears bleak and meaningless, a little gratitude goes a long way.

Write a detailed thank-you letter. Think of someone who has been especially kind to you—a friend, a teacher, a coworker—whom you've never properly thanked. Write a letter thanking this person, being specific about what he or she did that affected your life. Then schedule a meeting, maybe over coffee or a drink, and deliver the letter in person. Don't tell the person what the meeting is about; let it be a surprise. This form of gratitude can have a long-lasting effect. One study showed that after writing and delivering a thank-you letter, people had increased levels of happiness even two months later.[3]

Gratitude also reduces anxiety.[4] Both worry and anxiety arise out of the possibility that something bad might happen. But the brain can only focus on so many things at once, so when you're thankful for the good things that might occur in the future, gratitude replaces those negative feelings, and the worry evaporates.

Improved Physical Health

One Swiss study of nearly a thousand people used questionnaires to determine the connection between people's levels of gratitude and their health. The study found that people who expressed more gratitude had better physical and psychological health, and they were more likely to engage in healthy activities.[5] Grateful people also showed more willingness to do something about poor health. The drive to change your current circumstances is most likely mediated by serotonin, because without adequate serotonin function, people tend to become resigned to their fates.

Gratitude Increases Social Support

As you'll learn in the next chapter, social support helps create an upward spiral, and gratitude actually increases social support. In one study, one group of subjects were asked to keep a weekly journal of things they were grateful for, and that group was compared with subjects in groups who kept either a journal of things that bothered them or just a neutral list of what happened.[6] Another group of subjects were asked to compare themselves to others. The researchers looked both at average college students and at people with chronic medical conditions, who have an increased risk of depression. The study found that gratitude increased participants' quality of life as a whole, made them more optimistic, reduced aches and pains, and actually made them exercise more. Importantly, it also helped them feel more connected with other people.

> **Ask for help.** Sometimes when you're feeling crappy, it's hard to focus on—or even remember—happier times. If you're having difficulty remembering happy events, talk to an old friend, look at photographs, or read older entries from your diary. This is another reason to keep a gratitude journal; it's something to look back on when things get tough.

In another study, a group of British researchers looked at people going through life transitions (in this case, starting college).[7] Life transitions mean uncertainty, which revs up the limbic system. And when your environment changes, your habits change, so if you're not careful, you can fall into a routine that isn't optimal. The study found, not surprisingly, that the students with higher levels of gratitude had decreased stress and lower levels of depression. As in the previous study, they also found that gratitude increased feelings of social support. So you start with gratitude, and you get more social support, which helps you feel better and have more to be grateful for—and onward and upward.

Gratitude's Effect on the Brain

While gratitude has many positive effects, not many studies look directly at its effect on the brain. We have to draw what inferences we can from the few existing studies and from ones examining similar concepts.

Gratitude Improves Activity in Dopamine Circuits

The benefits of gratitude start with the dopamine system, because feeling grateful activates the brain stem region that produces dopamine.[8] Additionally, gratitude toward others increases activity in social dopamine circuits, which makes social interactions more enjoyable.

Keep a gratitude journal. Take a few minutes every day to write down three things you're grateful for. To make it a better habit, try doing it at the same time every day. If you can't think of three things, just write one. If you can't think of even one thing, just write, "I'm grateful for the food I ate today" or "I'm grateful for the clothes I'm wearing." Even if a situation is 90 percent what you don't want, you can still be grateful for the other 10 percent.

Gratitude Boosts Serotonin

One powerful effect of gratitude is that it can boost serotonin. Trying to think of things to be grateful for forces you to focus on the positive aspects of your life. This simple act increases serotonin production in the anterior cingulate cortex.[9] The same study that found this also showed that remembering sad events decreases serotonin production in the anterior cingulate. Thus, remembering positive events has a twofold effect: it directly increases serotonin and indirectly keeps you from remembering negative events.

Gratitude Improves Sleep

Gratitude is a great way to start an upward spiral, because it can improve your sleep—and we know from chapter 7 how important that is. A Canadian study took a group of college students with insomnia and asked them to keep a daily gratitude journal for a week.[10] This simple intervention led to improved sleep, reduced physical problems, and less worrying. Even in people with chronic pain,[11] gratitude improves sleep and reduces anxiety and depression.

Gratitude for the Future

Optimism combats negativity and is a form of gratitude, because we are grateful for the *possibility* of good things to come. We know from fMRI experiments that optimism is mediated by the ventral anterior cingulate,[12] and thus the ventral anterior cingulate likely plays a role in gratitude as well. With optimism, you don't even have to believe good things will happen; you just have to believe that they *could* happen or that no matter what happens, you'll be okay. In that case, optimism is being grateful for your resilience. Even if you think that you will mostly fall apart, there is some part of you that can endure any conditions—what Albert Camus called your "invincible summer." You can always access the upward spiral of gratitude.

Be grateful when you wake up. When you wake up in the morning, try to think of one thing you are looking forward to that day, even if it's just breakfast.

Compassion and admiration are similar to gratitude, and these too activate the anterior cingulate, as well as the insula and hypo-thalamus.[13] Since the insula reflects internal sensation, activation of the insula is likely a projection of empathy: feeling what someone else feels. The hypothalamus activity is a symptom of increased emotional arousal. The gratitude we feel toward other people likely has a similar effect on the brain.

Humor Appreciation

Appreciation is another variant of gratitude. While there haven't been many studies of gratitude's effect on the brain, there have been several studies of appreciation, specifically an apprecia-tion of humor.

Scientifically, there are two parts to getting a joke. The first part is recognizing that something is intended to be funny, and the second is actually "getting the joke" and appreciating the humor, which is often accompanied by laughter or a smile.

By looking at brain activity while subjects read cartoons, scien-tists can distinguish recognition and appreciation. It turns out that appreciating humor activates the orbitofrontal cortex, as well as the amygdala.[14] Humor-related amygdala activation illustrates that amygdala activation is not always bad—it's important to have an emotionally responsive limbic system, but for well-being, it's ideal to have it in balance.

Another study showed that humor appreciation also activates the dopamine-rich nucleus accumbens, as well as the brain stem region that produces dopamine,[15] which explains the enjoyable aspect of humor. It also activates areas of the dorsal striatum, which suggests that there is something habitual about humor appreciation. It is something you can practice, something you can get better at. At the very least, you now have a scientific reason to watch funny videos on YouTube.

The Powerful Pull of Guilt

An old Cherokee legend tells of a battle between two wolves. One wolf represents anger, jealousy, self-pity, sorrow, guilt, and resentment. The other stands for joy, peace, love, hope, kindness, and truth. It is a battle raging inside us all. Which wolf wins? The one you feed.

Pride, guilt, and shame are all self-focused, morally evaluative emotions. But while feeling proud of yourself is a cousin of gratitude, guilt and shame are the flip side. Since gratitude is so good for us, why is there such a strong pull toward shame and guilt in depression?

Despite their differences, pride, shame, and guilt all activate similar neural circuits, including the dorsomedial prefrontal cortex, amygdala, insula, and the nucleus accumbens.[16] Interestingly, pride is the most powerful of these emotions at triggering activity in these regions—except in the nucleus accumbens, where guilt and shame win out. This explains why it can be so appealing to heap guilt and shame on ourselves—they're activating the brain's reward center. Unfortunately, while guilt and shame might be reinforced in the brain, they're not beneficial to our long-term well-being. It's the same with food: candy bars may activate the nucleus accumbens more than fruit, but they're not in our long-term best interest. Feed your brain with gratitude instead, and it will nourish you with the benefits.

Don't Compare Yourself to Others

While trying to be grateful, it might be enticing to simply compare yourself to people who are less fortunate. Sure, you might not have a new car, but some people don't have a car at all. This may seem like the same thing as gratitude, but it's not. And studies show that comparing yourself to the less fortunate does not have the same benefits as gratitude.[17]

Gratitude is showing actual appreciation for the things you have. It does not matter what other people do or do not have. Gratitude is powerful because it decreases envy and increases how much you value what you already have, which improves life satisfaction.[18]

> **Take a deep breath.** A nice long one, through your nose. At the top of your breath, pause for a moment to think, "I am grateful for this breath," then let it out slowly.

Furthermore, comparing yourself to others activates circuits responsible for social comparison. Sure, you might come out favorably in some scenarios, but definitely not in all scenarios. In addition, the way your brain determines how other people think is that it takes what it's thinking and projects it outward. If you do lots of social comparisons, you're more likely to assume other people are engaging in social comparisons about you, and that can make you feel judged and excluded.

On the other hand, showing gratitude, kindness, and compassion toward others activates more positive social circuits. And when you feel these emotions toward other people, you're more likely to assume that other people are feeling the same about you.

The Difference Between Fishing and Catching

Once, while at a Boy Scout camp, I saw an old scoutmaster heading down to the lake with a rod and reel. A couple hours later, as he was walking back, I asked him how the fishing was. "Great," he responded. "How much did you catch?" I asked. "I didn't catch anything," he replied, adding, "It's called 'fishing,' not 'catching.'"

You can't always find something to be grateful for, but just because you can't find it doesn't mean it's useless to look. It's not finding gratitude that matters most; it's remembering to look in the first place.

Remembering to be grateful is a form of emotional intelligence. One study found that it actually affected neuron density in both the ventromedial and lateral prefrontal cortex.[19] These density changes suggest that as emotional intelligence increases, the neurons in these areas become more efficient. With higher emotional intelligence, it simply takes less effort to be grateful.

With gratitude, it is often the searching, the looking, the fishing for gratitude that activates the circuitry. You can't control what you see, but you can control what you're looking for. Sure, finding something to be grateful for is an added bonus, but it's not the only thing.

Chapter 11

Rely on the Power
of Others

A few years ago I spoke with a college student with severe depression. He said that when it really got bad, he only wanted to be alone in his dorm room. Even if he could still manage to study, he just wanted to be alone. And as he sat by himself, he would feel worse and worse until he couldn't even study; instead, he'd just lie in bed doing nothing.

Fortunately, he began to recognize this pattern in himself. He realized that even though he wanted to be alone, it wasn't good for him. From that point on, when he felt the pull toward isolation, he forced himself to go downstairs and do his homework in the lounge with other people bustling about. He didn't force himself to talk to anyone; he just made sure he was around other people. And that was enough to keep him from slipping further into a downward spiral.

Depression is an isolating disease. It makes you feel separate and alone, even around other people, and this often makes people want to be physically separate. But that desire for solitude is just a symptom of the depressed brain, and it perpetuates the disease, just as the desire to not exercise perpetuates it. One of the most important neuroscience principles to take from this book is that even though you may feel like being alone, the cure to depression often lies in other people.

> **Be around people.** Downward spirals are more likely when you're alone. If you start to feel your mood sliding downhill, try going somewhere where there are other people around, like a library or coffee shop. You don't need to interact with others; just being in the same physical space can help.

Humans are a social species—we evolved to survive with each other, and our brains are healthiest when we interact with and feel connected to others. That means that when we feel disconnected, the consequences can be devastating. Fortunately, research has clearly demonstrated that interacting with others—and not just friends and family but strangers too (and even pets)—can reverse the course of depression. Social interactions change the activity of numerous brain circuits and neurotransmitter systems. Talking, physical contact, or even just being near other people can decrease stress, pain, anxiety, and depressive symptoms, and it can increase calmness and happiness. We'll get to all the good stuff shortly, but first we'll talk about why it's often difficult to embrace this idea.

The Trouble with Other People

The poet Emily Dickinson once wrote, "It might be lonelier without the loneliness." She famously kept to herself and yet was scared of being alone. This apparent paradox is common, because the people who most yearn for closeness are often the most sensitive to rejection. Whether you have depression or not, other people can often be a source of stress and anxiety.

Our brains are wired to care what people think about us, which is why feeling judged or rejected is so distressing. In fact, as demonstrated in an fMRI experiment, social exclusion activates the same circuitry as physical pain.[1] In the experiment, participants were scanned while playing a virtual ball-tossing game with two other players. They were told the others were real people, but in fact, it was computer controlled. At first the "other players" played nicely, sharing the ball with the participant. But at one point they stopped sharing, only throwing back and forth to each other, ignoring the participant. This small change was enough to elicit feelings of social exclusion, and it activated the anterior cingulate and insula, just like physical pain would. We avoid social exclusion for the same reason we avoid touching a hot stove: it hurts!

Reflecting on rejection. We often experience something as rejection when it's really just a misunderstanding. For example, maybe you leave a message for a friend, and he or she doesn't call you back. It's easy to assume the intention was to hurt you or that your friend doesn't care enough about you. But those are not the only options. A more likely scenario is that your friend got too busy and forgot—or just missed the message in the first place. Thinking of alternate possibilities activates the medial prefrontal cortex—improving emotional regulation over the limbic system and helping you feel better. Sometimes asking the friend to clarify his or her intentions can be helpful. Furthermore, recognize that feelings of social rejection are enhanced by a bad mood or depression. So however bad it seems, it's not really that bad.

Interestingly, people with low self-esteem have even greater anterior cingulate activation, suggesting their brains are more sensitive to social rejection.[2] And in depression too, the brain tends to have greater sensitivity to social rejection, generating a stronger stress response.[3] Now, increased sensitivity to social rejection is not inherently a bad thing. In fact, it's often what creates group harmony, because it makes people want to fit in. However, like many traits mentioned in this book, it puts you at risk for a downward spiral.

When other people have the power to hurt you, it makes sense that you'd want to be alone sometimes. It's a perfectly reasonable coping mechanism and fine in moderation. But unfortunately, like eating ice cream to cope with stress, it might make you feel better momentarily, but it doesn't solve the problem. And in depression, the problem goes even deeper than that.

Depression Disrupts the Neurochemistry of Love and Trust

When it comes to love and intimate relationships, one neurohormone gets more press than anything else. Its name is *oxytocin* and it's often called the "love hormone." Oxytocin is released during light caresses and sex, when someone shows they trust you, and sometimes simply during conversation, which increases feelings of trust and attachment for others. Oxytocin also decreases feelings of stress, fear, and pain.

Unfortunately, in depression, the oxytocin system is out of sorts. Some studies say that people with depression have more oxytocin, and other studies say they have less. While this seems paradoxical, oxytocin levels influence—and are influenced by—different subtypes of depression,[4] reflecting the idea that each individual's specific neural circuits interact to create a unique instance of depression. So while the studies aren't exactly clear, the easiest way to understand it is to say that the whole oxytocin system is just out of whack. The proper biological term is *dysregulated*. In depression, oxytocin isn't always released when it should be, and it's sometimes released when it shouldn't.[5] In addition, the brain's response to oxytocin isn't always on target.

Even if the studies aren't clear about the overall function of oxytocin in depression, some studies illuminate its role in more narrow contexts. For example, people with lower levels of oxytocin are more likely to feel like life isn't worth living.[6] And many people at risk for depression, such as survivors of childhood abuse, have lower levels of oxytocin.[7] Genetics clearly plays a role as well. Certain genes that regulate the oxytocin system can increase levels of depression and anxiety.[8] In addition, people with depression are more likely to have a particular gene for the oxytocin receptor that causes decreased confidence in social relationships and an increased need for approval.[9] Interestingly, this connection between genes and relationships was seen only in people with depression, not in healthy controls—who had the same genes, but no depression—which suggests there is nothing inherently bad about these genes. But once a downward spiral starts, genetics can contribute to it.

Additionally, the pleasure that depressed people take from social interactions correlates with oxytocin levels.[10] That is, depressed people with lower levels of oxytocin take less enjoyment from social approval and support. Unfortunately, that's a potential downward spiral, because if you don't find social interaction rewarding, you're less likely to socialize, which will lead to even lower levels of oxytocin.

Impressively though, oxytocin can play a role in preventing depression in the first place. One fascinating study allowed mice to recover from a small injury either by themselves or in pairs.[11] Mice recovering by themselves were more likely to develop depressive symptoms and give up easily on difficult tasks, while mice with a partner showed less depression and more fortitude. And the researchers were able to show that the antidepressant effects in the paired mice were caused by elevated oxytocin.

So in general, disruptions of oxytocin and frontal-limbic circuitry create the potential for a downward spiral because they reduce connectedness. Fortunately, other people can help you improve both your oxytocin system and your frontal-limbic circuitry to reverse the course of depression.

What Other People Can Do for You and Your Brain

Interacting with others can help reduce your pain, anxiety, and stress, and and it can improve your mood. These benefits come from boosts in oxytocin and by changing fronto-limbic communication. Even when other people don't help you feel better right away, interacting with others pushes the brain in the right direction.

Reduce Pain and Discomfort

Nobody wants to stick his or her hand in a bucket of ice water and leave it there until the pain is overwhelming, but that's exactly what participants of one study were asked to do.[12] Some participants had to sit by themselves, while others were allowed to sit with a stranger or even a friend. The participants sitting by themselves experienced much greater levels of pain, while having a friend say supportive things greatly reduced the pain. Even just having the friend sit there saying nothing reduced the pain. In fact, even having a total stranger voice support or just passively sit with the participant caused the same benefits.

This same effect is seen in patients with chronic pain. In one study, patients who had their significant other present experienced greatly reduced sensations of pain.[13] Surprisingly, sometimes even just thinking about a loved one is enough to reduce pain.[14] Even more surprisingly, the same is true for talking to a stranger.[15] Pain is an internal sensation and is heightened when you focus on it.

Because talking with other people activates prefrontal social circuitry, it can help shift the brain's focus away from pain.

In addition, holding hands with someone can help comfort you and your brain through painful situations. One fMRI study scanned married women as they were warned that they were about to get a small electric shock.[16] While anticipating the painful shocks, the brain showed a predictable pattern of response in pain and worrying circuits, with activation in the insula, anterior cingulate, and dorsolateral prefrontal cortex. During a separate scan, the women either held their husbands' hands or the hand of the experimenter. When a subject held her husband's hand, the threat of shock had a smaller effect. The brain showed reduced activation in both the anterior cingulate cortex and dorsolateral prefrontal cortex—that is, less activity in the pain and worrying circuits. In addition, the stronger the marriage, the lower the discomfort-related insula activity. But even just holding the hand of the experimenter—a stranger—reduced activation in the anterior cingulate so that the women felt less distressed about the shocks.

Friends, Family, and Strangers Improve Your Mood

Depression often makes you want to be alone, but in fact, spending time with friends and relatives eases a depressed mood.[17] Surprisingly, the support of friends and family even improves the effects of antidepressant medications.[18] People who have more social support before they start taking medication are more likely to experience a reduction in their symptoms and also more likely to get completely better. In addition, the same study showed that as people's symptoms improved, their social support did too. So being social helps you get better, and getting better helps you be more social—another upward spiral.

Do an activity with a friend. Often when you're depressed, you don't feel like talking. Try an activity in which you can engage with someone but won't feel pressured to talk. Go see a movie or play a board game. You won't feel forced to talk about your depression if you don't want to, but there will be opportunities to open up if you feel like it.

Even talking to strangers can help. One study in Chicago paid bus and train commuters to either strike up a conversation with a stranger or just sit quietly.[19] The results showed that talking with a stranger led to better moods. In fact, while most people were worried that talking with a stranger would be unpleasant, after doing so, they actually had a happier commute. So try talking to the person next to you on a plane or in line with you at Starbucks. Sure, you might be apprehensive, but chances are, it'll be a positive experience.

The effect of social interaction on mood and medication is likely due to the fact that the oxytocin system supports the serotonin system. Many serotonin-producing neurons have receptors for oxytocin, so when oxytocin is released, it increases release of serotonin.[20] Thus oxytocin helps provide the benefits of serotonin that we've covered in earlier chapters.

Ease Stress and Anxiety

Interacting with friends also helps reduce stress and anxiety. One study looked at the stress levels of participants before public speaking. Some participants were allowed to hang out with a friend beforehand, and others were not. The results showed that talking with a friend reduced levels of stress hormones and feelings of anxiety, and it increased feelings of calmness.[21] Stressful situations are almost always easier to deal with when supportive people are present.

These effects are likely caused by changes to the amygdala and hippocampus. When the amygdala becomes too reactive, your stress response goes off at the slightest provocation, like a gunslinger with an itchy trigger finger. Fortunately, oxytocin reduces the twitchiness of the amygdala.[22] Oxytocin also increases the communication between the amygdala, prefrontal cortex, and anterior cingulate.[23] Lowering amygdala reactivity and strengthening frontal-limbic circuitry helps you regulate your emotions so that they're not wildly out of control.

In addition, we know that stress is bad for the hippocampus and can actually make it lose neurons. Fortunately, oxytocin helps protect the brain against the harmful effects of stress. And, like both exercise and antidepressant medication, oxytocin causes growth of new neurons in the hippocampus,[24] even in times of stress. So during stressful times you can utilize oxytocin to keep your brain healthy, and we're about to learn exactly how to do that.

Social Support Counteracts Social Rejection

Social support comes in many forms—even text messages, Facebook comments, and emails can help counteract feelings of social rejection. In one study involving the same virtual ball-tossing game described previously, the participants—after feeling socially excluded in the game—received emotionally supportive messages from the experimenters.[25] That emotional support reduced discomfort-related insula activity and increased activity in both the lateral and medial prefrontal areas. These results suggest that emotional support enhances prefrontal activity, which may weaken the limbic system's response. So even if it feels like the whole world is against you, having just one person on your side can make a big difference.

Be grateful. Remember that gratitude can improve feelings of social support (chapter 10)? Once a week, write down the things you're grateful for. This simple intervention is enough to help you feel more connected with others.

Help Yourself by Helping Others

In addition to friends and family, volunteering to help others also improves symptoms of depression and increases positive emotions.[26] So helping other people can be a great way to help yourself. One reason for this is likely the activation of empathy circuits in the brain. Empathy requires medial prefrontal involvement and thus can positively affect frontal-limbic communication. Interestingly, the effect is most pronounced in older adults. So if you're getting near retirement—or are well past it—volunteering can have a big impact on your depression.

Importantly, if you're having difficulty being happy, it can be easier to absorb feelings of happiness from others than to generate them in yourself. Levels of happiness are contagious; they can spread through a social network like the common cold.[27] After examining over four thousand people for twenty years, Harvard researchers found that if you have a friend who lives nearby who becomes happy, your chances of becoming happy increase by 25 percent. And if your next-door neighbor becomes happy, the effect is 34 percent.

Enjoyment, Addiction, and Oxytocin

Being around other people and developing close relationships feels good for a reason, and that reason is dopamine. Thus it's not surprising that dopamine and oxytocin interact with each other. Dopamine neurons connect to the part of the hypothalamus where oxytocin is produced,[28] and oxytocin stimulates the area of the brain stem where dopamine is produced. In addition, the dopamine-rich nucleus accumbens receives input from oxytocin neurons. Unfortunately, when oxytocin isn't working properly, its proper interactions with dopamine are disrupted, and thus social interactions aren't always as enjoyable. But given its benefits, even if interacting with others doesn't always feel amazing, it's still crucial to do it regularly.

The interaction of oxytocin and dopamine also helps explain one of the problems with addiction. Over time, drugs of abuse, such as cocaine, dramatically lower oxytocin levels in several key areas, including the hippocampus, hypothalamus, and nucleus accumbens.[29] These reductions explain why addiction gets in the way of forming and maintaining close, healthy relationships. In fact, oxytocin can help reduce addiction. Oxytocin reduces the nucleus accumbens response to drugs of abuse[30]—that is, oxytocin makes them less addicting. It can also reduce alcohol consumption.[31]

Activating Social Circuits

There are many ways to increase oxytocin or, generally, to activate brain circuits involved in being social. These often involve various forms of touching, like hugs and handshakes and massage. Talking with people—and sometimes just being around other people—also activates the social brain and can release oxytocin. Even pets can help release oxytocin.

Hugs and Handshakes

One of the primary ways to release oxytocin is through touching.[32] Obviously, it's not always appropriate to touch most people, but small touches like handshakes and pats on the back are usually okay. For people you're close with, make more of an effort to touch more often. Hugs, especially long ones, are particularly good at releasing oxytocin (and so are orgasms).

Turn up the heat. Feeling warm can boost oxytocin—or at least mimic its effects, increasing feelings of trust and generosity.[33] So if you can't get a hug, try wrapping yourself in a blanket and holding a mug of hot tea. Taking a warm shower can also help.

Massage

Massage reduces pain because the oxytocin system activates painkilling endorphins.[34] Massage also improves sleep and reduces fatigue[35] by increasing serotonin and dopamine and decreasing the stress hormone cortisol.[36] So if you're feeling out of sorts, get a massage. You'll be actively triggering the neurotransmitter systems that work to make you happier.

Interacting with Friends

Individuals who interact regularly with a supportive friend, family member, or colleague are more resilient to stress.[37] The study that demonstrated this also showed that decreased stress was linked to diminished activity in the dorsal anterior cingulate, which suggests that it was less focused on the negative.

Talking with friends helps reduce stress, likely by increasing oxytocin.[38] However, while some people find conversations relaxing, others require greater medial prefrontal processing during face-to-face conversations and may find them tiring.[39] The more agreeable you are, the less prefrontal effort required. So if you find that talking to people feels effortful, try being more agreeable or supportive and less argumentative or judgmental.

Talk to people you care about. That doesn't mean stalk them on Facebook. Email them. Call them. Even better, go for a walk with them or meet for coffee—do something fun.

When it comes to reducing stress, not all forms of "talking" are created equal. One study brought eight- to twelve-year-old girls into the lab and asked them to solve difficult SAT questions in front of an audience.[40] Needless to say, this was a bit stressful. Afterward, the girls were assigned to one of four groups. The first three groups were allowed either to visit with their mothers, talk with them over the phone, or text them; the fourth group was not allowed any contact at all. Girls who were allowed to visit with or talk with their mothers had reduced cortisol and increased oxytocin. In contrast, girls who were not allowed any contact had high levels of cortisol and low levels of oxytocin. Interestingly, the text-message group had cortisol and oxytocin levels similar to the no-contact group. Thus, there is something comforting about verbal speech that is not always captured in a text message.

Root for a sports team. One of the most powerful ways to combat depression is a sense of belonging. Winning is fun, even if you're just a spectator. Cheering for a winning sports team increases testosterone,[41] which boosts energy and sex drive. A sports team also provides a community, so even after losses, you have the camaraderie—and there's always the hope that your team will win next time.

Sometimes even just thinking about people can be helpful. In a Dutch study, participants were asked to think about someone they felt close to, someone they would go to if they had a problem.[42] They were asked to imagine that person standing behind them being supportive, and they were then taken through an experiment intended to create feelings of social exclusion. Thinking about a close friend reduced reactivity in the hypothalamus, the region responsible for the stress response. Furthermore, feelings of connectedness strengthened activity in both the medial and dorsolateral prefrontal cortex, giving people a greater sense of control over their life and their emotions.

Man's Best Friend

Members of the armed services returning from Iraq and Afghanistan are five times more likely to suffer from depression than the average civilian. But giving them a dog can help tremendously, and it can help civilians too. Several studies have shown that pets reduce depression; they change your focus, habits, and biofeedback, and they also boost oxytocin and other neurotransmitters.

Taking a dog for a walk can be beneficial as well. In one study, Japanese researchers hooked participants up to a portable EKG machine so they could monitor their heart-rate variability while they walked a dog.[43] Remember that heart-rate variability is lower in depression, and that increasing your heart-rate variability can help improve depression through biofeedback (see chapter 9). The study found that when participants were given a dog to walk, their heart-rate variability increased significantly. In addition, even while sitting at home afterward, the dog-walkers had elevated heart-rate variability.

A different Japanese study showed that playing with a dog with which you have a strong bond—a dog that is more likely to make eye contact with you—can increase oxytocin.[44] This suggests that having someone look to you for support or trust can increase oxytocin. Simply petting a dog can also start an upward spiral. Petting, like other forms of light touch, boosts oxytocin. And petting a dog, even someone else's dog, also increases dopamine and endorphins.[45] The increases in these other neurotransmitters provides even more thrust to an upward spiral.

An important component of the antidepressant effect of pets may not necessarily come from walking or playing, but simply from being responsible for another living creature. One study showed that when elderly residents of a retirement home had a canary to take care of, they had lower levels of depression.[46] When you have something you're responsible for, it helps maintain your focus, and it impacts your habits.

Lastly, pets not only increase oxytocin directly but also promote social interactions with other people. This is called the "social catalyst effect"—walking a dog increases the chances that a random stranger will smile at you or even start talking to you.[47] So pets can increase positive interactions with other people, creating an upward spiral of socializing that will combat feelings of loneliness and isolation.

Some Things to Watch Out For

Creating an upward spiral with oxytocin is not always a smooth road, but knowing the potential obstacles can make you better prepared to deal with them.

Oxytocin and Sex Hormones

Oxytocin neurons are sensitive to rapidly changing levels of sex hormones, such as estrogen or testosterone.[48] When sex hormone levels jump or drop, oxytocin neurons can stop working smoothly. Because these hormones change dramatically after pregnancy and during adolescence, the related changes in oxytocin may contribute to postpartum depression as well as depression in teenagers. Sex hormone levels can also be affected by social status—losing your job can have a negative hormonal impact. Lastly, sex hormones also change at the beginning of relationships and after breakups. Being aware of the oxytocin system's sensitivity can hopefully help you be more proactive in preventing a downward spiral. Utilize the suggestions in this chapter, like exercise and hugs. Remember to hang out with friends or even ask them to occasionally check on how you're doing. Make a habit of calling your family once a week. If anxiety starts to rumble inside you, practice the mindfulness techniques discussed in chapter 2. Lastly, even simply being aware that your emotions may be exaggerated by fluctuating oxytocin can help you feel more in control of the situation.

Oxytocin Isn't Always Easy

Unfortunately, oxytocin does not cure everyone's problems immediately, and achieving the benefits of oxytocin may take work. Oxytocin increases feelings of bonding, but that doesn't always decrease stress. Stress goes up when things are out of your control, and when you care strongly for someone else, your life can often feel out of control (the tips in chapter 2 can help). On top of that, caring about someone can increase insula reactivity—your loved one's distress affects you more viscerally.[49] It's great to feel empathy, but sometimes watching the people you care about suffering can be overwhelming.

Continuing with the less-than-great news: it turns out that if you didn't have a good relationship with your parents, it's harder to harness the positive effects of oxytocin. One recent study looked at the response of women to hearing a baby cry. These women were given puffs of oxytocin while being asked to grip a bar.[50] Women who had not been disciplined harshly as children relaxed their grip when they heard the baby cry, presumably as preparation to gently comfort the baby. Women who had been disciplined harshly as children, however, did not relax their grip. So if you received harsh discipline as a child, oxytocin does not automatically create conditions for warm, gentle interactions.

In addition, oxytocin enhances your feelings about close relationships based on your relationship with your parents. For example, in a recent study researchers gave men a small puff of oxytocin and asked them to think about their mothers.[51] After oxytocin, men who had a positive relationship with their mothers remembered that relationship as even more positive. But for those who had difficult maternal relationships, they remembered them as even worse. So if you had a tough relationship with your parents, your brain may have a tendency to react to close relationships in a negative way.

That might seem like a raw deal, because you can't change your childhood, but fortunately, long-term changes to the oxytocin system are possible. Oxytocin neurons go through structural changes when they're stimulated. With regular stimulation, the changes can last for months,[52] leading to long-term alterations in their firing patterns.[53] Anything you do to stimulate oxytocin can help improve the whole system. The brain operates largely on a use-it-or-lose-it basis, and oxytocin is no different—it can be exercised and strengthened just like your cardiovascular system.

Because it can be scary when you first start reaching out to people, seeing a therapist can help (see chapter 12), just as having a personal trainer can help when you start working out. Just remember, whether or not oxytocin makes you feel good immediately, it's nonetheless changing your brain's chemical and electrical activity. Find a community where you feel like you belong—a church, a team, or an activity group. Keep seeking interactions with others, and be patient with yourself—allow your brain time to rewire.

Chapter 12

Your Brain in Therapy

W hen you need to remodel your kitchen, you call a contractor. If your car needs a new transmission, you take it to a mechanic. For almost any specialized job, there's a professional who can help. Maybe one isn't always necessary, but professionals often get the job done better and faster. Yet many people with depression are unwilling to seek professional help.

While most of this book has been about how to help yourself, I don't mean to downplay the power of professional help. Psychiatrists and psychologists are another part of the upward spiral. They're an additional tool to help modify the circuits in your brain and improve your access to happiness, increase your focus, and reduce stress, anxiety, and depression. And they can be more than just a tool. They can be coaches as well—helping you help yourself and providing even more tools to help you get better.

Aside from psychotherapy, modern science has developed numerous methods to boost your brain and reverse the course of depression. Antidepressant medications are a great start, but there are also other helpful treatments. Letting medical and mental health professionals do their job can help your efforts to reshape your brain.

Professional Help Helps

There are many effective treatments for depression that can work wonders. The problem is, they're not all completely effective on everyone. If one hundred depressed people take medication for a few months, about thirty of them will get fully better.[1] That's not an amazing cure rate, but it's still thirty people who overcame depression by doing nothing more than taking a pill. Another twenty people will get substantially better, but will still be somewhat depressed. Unfortunately, the rest will only get slightly better or stay the same. But if those last fifty people try a different medication, another fifteen get better. With a third medication, a few more will get better.

For psychotherapy alone, the numbers are about the same as the first round of medication, with about half overcoming depression or getting substantially better. And if you combine medication with psychotherapy, the chances of getting better almost double.[2]

Yes, not knowing if a particular treatment will work can be frustrating. However, like everything else in this book, the amount that a particular life change will help is almost always unknown. For some people, a little exercise goes a long way. For others, simply changing sleep patterns can work wonders. Some people need Prozac; others need Wellbutrin. It all depends on the unique tuning of your neural circuits. You can't really know which kind of brain you have until you give it a try.

One drawback to these treatments is that they can sometimes take a few weeks to start working. When the cure doesn't happen immediately, people often stop, particularly with medication. But that's not a good strategy. You can't go to the gym for a week and conclude, "Exercise doesn't help me." It may take a few months to get in shape. The same is true of treatments for depression. In one of the largest studies of depression treatment ever done, half the people who got fully better took over six weeks to do so. Many people took even longer, but still got there.[3] So be patient with your treatment. Even if it doesn't work at first, it may start to kick in later. The one thing you can be sure of is that even if you don't feel better, the medication is having positive effects on your brain. Feeling better is simply a combination of finding the right life changes for you to create the right brain changes. Everyone's brain is different, and everyone's depression is different, so treatment is often an exploration.

How Psychotherapy Changes the Brain

How much can talking with someone really change your brain? A lot. In the last chapter, we discussed the benefits of support from friends and loved ones, but talking to a professional can have its own benefits. That's not to say a therapist is a replacement for friends and family but rather that therapists have their own unique contribution.

Psychotherapy Reduces Limbic Reactivity

As I've explained since the beginning of this book, depression is a dysfunction in frontal-limbic communication—and psychotherapy is a great treatment because it normalizes limbic activity.

In one German study, people with depression underwent longer-term psychoanalysis, which is a form of Freudian psychotherapy that deals with symbols and the childhood origins of current problems.[4] At the beginning and then after a year of psychoanalysis, the patients had fMRI scans, during which they were shown pictures that aroused feelings of isolation or difficulty connecting with others. Before therapy, compared to controls, the depressed group had elevated medial prefrontal cortex activity, indicating excessive self-focused, emotional processing of the images. After therapy, medial prefrontal activity went back down to the levels of healthy controls. Furthermore, the limbic system came back under control, with reduced reactivity in the amygdala, hippocampus, and ventral anterior cingulate. So psychotherapy succeeded in eliminating the depressed pattern of activity.

Go see a professional. Make an appointment with a psychiatrist, psychologist, or therapist. They've undergone years of training to help people like you. Maybe you doubt that a professional will help; but like almost every other aspect of the upward spiral, while you can't be certain that any solution will definitely work, you can be certain that if you don't try, nothing is likely to change.

A study from Duke treated depression for six months with cognitive-behavioral therapy, which is a form of therapy that attempts to change maladaptive thoughts and behaviors. Participants also underwent fMRI scanning before and after treatment.[5] The scan before treatment showed that people with depression had limbic systems that did not discriminate well between emotional and neutral information; the depressed brain treated all information the same, regardless of whether it was emotional or not. As you may remember from chapter 3, this type of response comes from an overactive limbic system and can contribute to a downward spiral. After treatment, the brain began to separate its response to emotional and nonemotional information, showing more appropriate discrimination in key limbic areas like the amygdala and hippocampus. Thus the balance in the frontal-limbic communication was restored.

Psychotherapy Increases Enjoyment in the Brain

In depression, it's common to find activities not as enjoyable or rewarding as they once were. Fortunately, it's possible to change that with *behavioral activation therapy* (BAT), which involves getting you to do activities that are likely to be enjoyable, meaningful, or useful, and to decrease behaviors that lead to downward spirals. For example, the "productive procrastination" discussed in chapter 8 is one application of BAT. It also includes forcing yourself to habitually do small useful tasks like taking a shower every morning or making the bed every day. (For more useful tips, check out www.flylady.net.) Even if you don't see the point or don't enjoy doing them, you're still accomplishing small goals and deriving the neural benefits that come with them.

In a study out of North Carolina, depressed subjects went through a couple months of BAT, then played a gambling game inside an fMRI scanner.[6] The study found that therapy increased the brain's response to reward, particularly in the orbitofrontal cortex, which is responsible for motivation. So if you're lacking motivation or don't find your usual hobbies enjoyable, BAT can help.

Do what you used to enjoy. It can be stressful if you don't enjoy hobbies or activities anymore, but you can overcome this with your own form of BAT. Make a list of things you used to enjoy (playing tennis, going to the movies with friends, and so on). Recognize that your lack of enjoyment is only a temporary situation and keep doing the things you used to enjoy, even if they don't seem as fun.

Importantly, BAT also increases dorsal striatum activity, which promotes doing enjoyable activities and good habits. Other treatments, like interpersonal psychotherapy and medication, also strengthen the dorsal striatum,[7] so there are many ways to restore your enjoyment of activities.

Psychotherapy Reduces Anxious Prefrontal Activity

In one study of psychotherapy's effects on the depressed brain, Canadian researchers compared cognitive-behavioral therapy and antidepressants.[8] The therapy included mindfulness techniques as well as behavioral activation. The study found that cognitive-behavioral therapy increased hippocampal activity and decreased prefrontal activity. The prefrontal deactivation was probably related to reduced activation of worrying circuits. Furthermore, these changes were distinct from those of medication. This suggests that psychotherapy and medication attack depression on different fronts.

In another Canadian study, researchers examined patients with moderate levels of anxiety and depression who were enrolled in a mindfulness-based stress reduction program.[9] Mindfulness training is not psychotherapy per se, but it includes many techniques from cognitive-behavioral therapy, so there's a lot of overlap. Subjects were taught to cultivate a mode of acceptance of their feelings. Often we don't want to feel our negative emotions, so we push them away. Unfortunately, that doesn't resolve them; it just leaves us with added frustration. Acceptance, on the other hand, teaches that how you feel is simply how you feel. It's neither good nor bad. It just is. And interestingly, when you're stewing in negative emotions, accepting them often helps them dissipate, like an early morning mist beneath a ray of sun.

After learning mindfulness skills over a series of classes, the subjects were shown sad clips from movies. Amazingly, their brains' response to sadness had changed, accompanied by significant reductions in their depression, anxiety, and physical symptoms. Mindfulness training reduced the usual deactivation in their insula and lateral prefrontal cortex so that they kept their same level of functioning, despite feeling sad. Lastly, mindfulness increased activity in the ventral anterior cingulate, which is the area that correlates with increased optimism. These nuanced changes in brain activity emphasize the intricate pattern that keeps the brain stuck in depression, and how disrupting that pattern is what the upward spiral is all about.

Psychotherapy Strengthens Serotonin

In one Finnish study, psychotherapy for depression increased the number of serotonin receptors in most of the prefrontal cortex.[10] This makes perfect sense, as prefrontal serotonin helps better regulate your emotions and impulses. Several parts of the attention circuit, including the anterior cingulate, also showed increases.

Though remember that psychotherapy works differently on different people's brains. Most people who get better with psychotherapy have significant increases in the number of serotonin transporter molecules,[11] but others will get better with no change in serotonin transporters. So psychotherapy works via different brain mechanisms in different people.

Psychotherapy Works Differently Than Medication

Not only does psychotherapy work differently for different people, it also acts on different circuits than medication does. The Finnish study previously described found that while psychotherapy caused numerous changes in serotonin receptors, medication had no such effect.[12] The participants on medication still had similar improvements in their depression; they just didn't have similar changes in serotonin receptors. Other studies show that psychotherapy causes changes in limbic activity that medication doesn't.[13] These results suggest that psychotherapy and medication work in different ways to cure depression. So if one doesn't work, maybe the other will. (And in fact, people often benefit most from combining psychotherapy and medication.)

How Antidepressant Medications Change the Brain

One of the easiest ways to kick-start an upward spiral is to take antidepressant medication, because it can have such wide-reaching effects on the brain.

How They Work

Different medications have slightly different mechanisms of action, but almost all work by affecting the serotonin, norepinephrine, and dopamine systems to varying degrees. One of the most common types of antidepressant medications is *selective serotonin reuptake inhibitors* (SSRIs). SSRIs include drugs like Lexapro, Prozac, Paxil, Celexa, and Zoloft. They bind to the *serotonin transporter*, a molecule that is responsible for sucking serotonin out of the synapse. Normally, serotonin gets squirted out into the synapse, where it can activate neighboring neurons, and the serotonin transporter quickly clears it away. But when you block the serotonin transporter, serotonin stays in the synapse longer and can have a stronger effect.

Other medications, such as Cymbalta and Pristiq, work more broadly, acting on both the serotonin and norepinephrine systems. And Wellbutrin works on a combination of the norepinephrine and dopamine systems.

Finding exactly which medication will work best for you is often a matter of trial and error, because the precise composition of your particular neurochemistry is unknown. Thus you might have to try a few medications before you find one that works well for you and doesn't give you unwanted side effects.

Their Effects on the Brain

Aside from the immediate effect of blocking transporters, antidepressants cause longer-term changes in the brain. They affect activity in numerous frontal and limbic areas, including the insula, hippocampus, amygdala, anterior cingulate, and dorsolateral prefrontal cortex. Furthermore, they cause new neurons to grow and have effects on numerous neurotransmitter systems, particularly dopamine and serotonin.

Antidepressants reduce reactivity in several limbic areas. In the amygdala, antidepressants lower the reactivity to emotional facial expressions,[14] even when you're not consciously aware of the emotions you're reacting to. In the insula, they reduce activity during times of uncertainty.[15] As you may recall from chapter 2, uncertainty increases worry and anxiety, even if you're anticipating positive outcomes. Antidepressants also decrease anterior cingulate activity, particularly in anticipation of negative events, which again reduces anxiety.

Antidepressants also diminish the anterior cingulate's response to pain,[16] meaning pain draws less of the anterior cingulate's attention. Being free from that distraction frees your brain to focus on more positive aspects of life.

Furthermore, antidepressants help restore proper frontal-limbic communication. Often in depression, emotions distract you from being able to concentrate and think clearly, but antidepressants fix that. They increase dorsolateral prefrontal activity while you're trying to focus and decrease reactivity from the amygdala, which distracts you from concentrating.[17]

They Have Many Neurochemical Effects

And then there's the neurochemistry of the brain. Antidepressants help the brain make fewer serotonin receptors, which modifies the serotonin system more permanently. Fewer serotonin receptors may not seem like a helpful change, but because so many brain regions interact in dynamic ways, a lot of what happens is not intuitive and not fully understood; this is one of them.

Surprisingly, as the brain reacts to the medication, in the first few weeks, it can actually slow the firing rate of serotonin neurons, which leads to lower serotonin levels.[18] Think of this like someone trying to get in shape for the first time in years; you're hoping to feel healthier, but the first few times you go to the gym, you feel worse. Then after a couple weeks, the firing rate of serotonin neurons recovers, and serotonin goes back up. The delayed recovery of serotonin neurons can help explain why medications often take a while to start working fully.

Even though most antidepressants don't directly target the dopamine system, they still can affect it. Antidepressants sensitize dopamine receptors, making them more sensitive to low levels of dopamine,[19] which helps make life more enjoyable and rewarding.

Antidepressants also cause increases in BDNF, which, as mentioned in previous chapters, is like fertilizer for the brain. It helps grow new neurons and rewire old ones, particularly in the prefrontal cortex and hippocampus, assisting with improved frontal-limbic communication.[20, 21] In contrast, stress slows down or stops new neurons from growing. So antidepressants can combat or even reverse the neural damage caused by stress.

Lastly, antidepressants also help improve quality sleep. They reduce the amount of REM sleep and increase the amount of more restorative slow-wave sleep.[22] In this respect, antidepressants have a similar effect to exercise, and we know that quality sleep contributes greatly to an upward spiral.

Brain Stimulation Techniques

In addition to psychotherapy and medication, the last few decades have seen a proliferation of other treatments to modify brain activity. These new treatments are various forms of *neuromodulation*, which is just a fancy word for "changing brain activity" or "brain stimulation." These techniques range from the proven to the experimental and from complex surgeries to completely noninvasive procedures. But the only way to find out if some neuromodulation procedure is right for you is to consult a mental-health professional.

Transcranial Magnetic Stimulation

Transcranial magnetic stimulation (TMS) is a technology that uses magnetic pulses to change neural activity. A technician places a strong, pulsing electromagnet over your dorsolateral prefrontal cortex—and that's basically it. It's a cool technology, because not only does it provide a direct way to influence brain circuitry, it just feels like someone gently tapping your forehead. A month of TMS treatment has proven helpful in combatting depression. TMS also affects regions that connect with the dorsolateral prefrontal cortex, including the dorsal striatum.[23] Regulation of the dorsal striatum means that people are better able to suppress old habits and create new behaviors. Furthermore, TMS increases dopamine release in the medial prefrontal cortex and the ventral anterior cingulate,[24] helping restore frontal-limbic balance.

Vagus Nerve Stimulation

Vagus nerve stimulation (VNS) is a technology that, as you may have guessed, stimulates the vagus nerve and helps treat depression. This requires an electrical stimulator surgically implanted in the neck, which proves prohibitive for some—though it might be worth it for patients with severe depression. VNS modifies brain activity via the vagus nerve in a similar manner to many of the biofeedback approaches discussed in chapter 9. While originally developed to treat epilepsy, VNS can help with depression, especially in the way the brain processes the sense of self.[25]

Electroconvulsive Therapy

Electroconvulsive therapy (ECT) is a technique in which electricity is delivered to the head in order to cause a therapeutic seizure. It was originally developed in the 1930s, when no psychiatric medications were available, and it quickly became clear that it was very effective for many patients with depression. It was less effective for other psychiatric disorders, but at the time, there were no alternatives. Unfortunately, in popular culture, ECT began to develop a negative reputation, fueled by negative media portrayals, such as *One Flew Over the Cuckoo's Nest,* which did not accurately depict the appropriate use of ECT. Since the 1950s, ECT has been used with anesthesia, so patients don't experience any pain or discomfort from the treatment. In the last few years, techniques have advanced even further to reduce side effects, and ECT has continually proven to be an extremely effective tool for treating severe depression.[26]

The exact reason ECT works is unknown, but it has broad effects on the brain. Similar to antidepressant medication, it increases BDNF, which helps grow new neurons.[27] ECT also increases oxytocin and improves serotonin receptor function, making them more sensitive, and it improves dopamine receptor function in the striatum.[28]

ECT is an FDA-approved procedure, but is generally performed only if less invasive therapies do not work. In the case that medication, psychotherapy, and life changes are not sufficient, ECT can be extremely effective at improving depression.

Future Techniques

The following two techniques have not yet been approved by the FDA, but I include them because they illustrate different ways of modifying the same circuits we've already discussed.

Transcranial direct current stimulation (tDCS) is a very simple technology that involves a couple of electrodes being placed on the scalp over the prefrontal cortex to deliver a very small electrical current. tDCS enhances dorsolateral prefrontal excitability, so the neurons there can activate more easily. One study of tDCS showed that most subjects reduced their symptoms by about 40 percent, and the benefits lasted for a month.[29] Those numbers certainly don't point to tDCS as a cure for depression, but it may be an easy way to help, if it gets FDA approval. And even though it has not been approved yet, because it is a relatively benign treatment, you may be able to find a psychiatrist who offers it "off label."

Lastly, for people with really severe depression, it can be helpful to surgically implant an electrode next to the ventral anterior cingulate.[30] This *deep brain stimulation* (DBS) directly modifies any circuits that involve the anterior cingulate, and in small studies, it has demonstrated a potentially dramatic impact on depression. However, it requires brain surgery, which is why this book suggests alternative ways to modulate the anterior cingulate.

Ultimately, there are dozens of ways to modify the brain circuits that create the downward spiral of depression. For some you need a prescription, for others you don't; but they are all a part of the upward spiral.

Conclusion

Our battered suitcases were piled on the sidewalk again; we had longer ways to go. But no matter, the road is life.

Jack Kerouac, *On the Road*

We've almost reached the end, and hopefully your suitcases are packed with a new understanding of your brain. You now know how various brain regions interact to create the downward spiral of depression, and you have the tools to do something about it.

You know that depression is a dysfunction in frontal-limbic communication. You know that the prefrontal cortex helps manage your emotions and desires so that you can plan for the future. The dorsal striatum acts out old habits, and the nucleus accumbens controls enjoyment and impulses. The anterior cingulate manages attention to the negative or the positive, and the insula is responsible for emotional sensations. The amygdala mediates anxiety. The hypothalamus regulates numerous hormones and controls the stress response. The hippocampus is closely tied to the amygdala and hypothalamus and is essential to learning and memory.

You also understand the contributions of the different neurotransmitters. Serotonin helps with impulse control, willpower, and resilience. Dopamine is important in enjoyment and habits. Norepinephrine modulates focus and concentration. Oxytocin is essential to close relationships. Other neurotransmitters are important too, like GABA (antianxiety), endorphins (elation and pain relief), and endocannabinoids (appetite and peacefulness). Other chemicals, like BDNF, help grow new neurons, and even proteins in the immune system play a role. The whole chemical milieu is as complicated and intertwined as international economics.

Everything is interconnected. Gratitude improves sleep. Sleep reduces pain. Reduced pain improves your mood. Improved mood reduces anxiety, which improves focus and planning. Focus and planning help with decision making. Decision making further reduces anxiety and improves enjoyment. Enjoyment gives you more to be grateful for, which keeps that loop of the upward spiral going. Enjoyment also makes it more likely you'll exercise and be social, which, in turn, will make you happier.

You now know dozens of ways to modulate all the important circuits. You can change dopamine and the dorsal striatum with exercise. You can boost serotonin with a massage. You can make decisions and set goals to activate the ventromedial prefrontal cortex. You can reduce amygdala activity with a hug and increase anterior cingulate activity with gratitude. You can enhance prefrontal norepinephrine with sleep. The list goes on and on, and these benefits create a feedback loop that causes even more positive changes.

The circuits in your brain are an interconnected web, like the environment; but it can be a fragile ecosystem sometimes. That's the problem with depression. It can set you spiraling downward, and everything becomes worse. However, with just a couple tiny life changes, you can reverse the trend. And as your brain starts to spiral upward, the ecosystem becomes more and more resilient, which helps prevent future bouts of depression.

Because all your neural circuits influence each other, the solution to your problems is not always straightforward. Don't feel like hanging out with people? Go for a run. Don't feel like doing work? Go outside. Can't sleep? Think about what you're grateful for. Worrying too much? Stretch.

Next time you're feeling down, just remember that it's your brain stuck in a certain pattern of activity. Do something to change the pattern—anything. Can't find a reason to get out of bed? Stop looking for a reason; just get out of bed. Once your hippocampus recognizes a changed context, it will trigger the dorsal striatum to start acting out habits, or at least trigger the prefrontal cortex to find a new reason. Go for a walk. Call a friend.

The End Is the Beginning

Congratulations! You've reached the end of the book. Even if you don't remember a thing, you've still reaped some neuroscientific benefits. Your brain is releasing dopamine even as you read these words, in anticipation of finishing; and when you're done and you close the book, it will release another puff of dopamine to help you go off into the world.

Thank you for reading. I hope something I've said has provided a new path toward getting better—or at least a bit of understanding and acceptance. Things might not seem different right away, but you've activated important circuits just by thinking about them. Whether it seems like it or not, your upward spiral is just beginning.

Acknowledgments

First, I'd like to thank my scientific mentors and supporters at UCLA: Mark Cohen, Andy Leuchter, Ian Cook, Michelle Abrams, and Alexander Bystritsky. Thanks to Angela Gorden and Jill Marsal for helping this book become a reality. Thanks to my family for their love and encouragement, particularly to my mother for her edits and neuroscience acumen. Thanks to Alex Thaler, Jessie Davis, Sam Torrisi, and Joey Cooper for their invaluable input. Thanks to Elizabeth Peterson for her love and support and for editing that makes me sound like I know how to write. And thanks to Bruin Ladies Ultimate for inspiring me through grad school and beyond.

Notes

Introduction

1. Coan, J. A., Schaefer, H. S., & Davidson, R. J. (2006). Lending a hand: Social regulation of the neural response to threat. *Psychological Science, 17*(12): 1032–1039.

2. Fumoto, M., Oshima, T., et al. (2010). Ventral prefrontal cortex and serotonergic system activation during pedaling exercise induces negative mood improvement and increased alpha band in EEG. *Behavioural Brain Research, 213*(1): 1–9.

3. Walch, J. M., Rabin, B. S., et al. (2005). The effect of sunlight on postoperative analgesic medication use: A prospective study of patients undergoing spinal surgery. *Psychosomatic Medicine, 67*(1): 156–163.

4. Fredrickson, B. L., & Joiner, T. (2002). Positive emotions trigger upward spirals toward emotional well-being. *Psychological Science, 13*(2): 172–175.

Chapter 1

1. American Psychiatric Association. (2000). *Diagnostic and statistical manual of mental disorders: DSM-IV-TR.* Washington, DC: American Psychiatric Association.

2. Schiepers, O. J., Wichers, M. C., & Maes, M. (2005). Cytokines and major depression. *Progress in Neuro-Psychopharmacology and Biological Psychiatry, 29*(2): 201–217.

3. Koenigs, M., & Grafman, J. (2009). The functional neuroanatomy of depression: Distinct roles for ventromedial and dorsolateral prefrontal cortex. *Behavioural Brain Research, 201*(2): 239–243.

4. Fu, C. H., Williams, S. C., et al. (2004). Attenuation of the neural response to sad faces in major depression by antidepressant treatment: A prospective, event-related functional magnetic resonance imaging study. *Archives of General Psychiatry, 61*(9): 877–889.

5. Buchanan, T. W. (2007). Retrieval of emotional memories. *Psychological Bulletin, 133*(5): 761–779.

6. MacQueen, G., & Frodl, T. (2011). The hippocampus in major depression: Evidence for the convergence of the bench and bedside in psychiatric research? *Molecular Psychiatry, 16*(3): 252–264.

7. Cooney, R. E., Joormann, J., et al. (2010). Neural correlates of rumination in depression. *Cognitive, Affective, & Behavioral Neuroscience, 10*(4): 470–478.

8. Korb, A. S., Hunter, A. M., et al. (2009). Rostral anterior cingulate cortex theta current density and response to antidepressants and placebo in major depression. *Clinical Neurophysiology, 120*(7): 1313–1319.

9. Mayberg, H. S., Lozano, A. M., et al. (2005). Deep brain stimulation for treatment-resistant depression. *Neuron, 45*(5): 651–660.

10. Wiebking, C., Bauer, A., et al. (2010). Abnormal body perception and neural activity in the insula in depression: An fMRI study of the depressed "material me." *World Journal of Biological Psychiatry, 11*(3): 538–549.

11. Pezawas, L., Meyer-Lindenberg, A., et al. (2005). 5-HTTLPR polymorphism impacts human cingulate-amygdala interactions: A genetic susceptibility mechanism for depression. *Nature Neuroscience, 8*(6): 828–834.

12. Talge, N. M., Neal, C., et al. (2007). Antenatal maternal stress and long-term effects on child neurodevelopment: How and why? *Journal of Child Psychology and Psychiatry, 48*(3–4): 245–261.

Chapter 2

1. Schwartz, B., Ward, A., et al. (2002). Maximizing versus satisficing: Happiness is a matter of choice. *Journal of Personality and Social Psychology, 83*(5): 1178–1197.

2. Hsu, M., Bhatt, M., et al. (2005). Neural systems responding to degrees of uncertainty in human decision-making. *Science, 310*(5754): 1680–1683.

3. Fincham, J. M., Carter, C. S., et al. (2002). Neural mechanisms of planning: A computational analysis using event-related fMRI. *Proceedings of the National Academy of Sciences USA, 99*(5): 3346–3351.

4. McLaughlin, K. A., Borkovec, T. D., & Sibrava, N. J. (2007). The effects of worry and rumination on affect states and cognitive activity. *Behavior Therapy, 38*(1): 23–38.

5. Paulesu, E., Sambugaro, E., et al. (2010). Neural correlates of worry in generalized anxiety disorder and in normal controls: A functional MRI study. *Psychological Medicine, 40*(1): 117–124.

6. Zebb, B. J., & Beck, J. G. (1998). Worry versus anxiety: Is there really a difference? *Behavior Modification, 22*(1): 45–61.

7. Sanderson, W. C., Rapee, R. M., & Barlow, D. H. (1989). The influence of an illusion of control on panic attacks induced via inhalation of 5.5% carbon dioxide-enriched air. *Archives of General Psychiatry, 46*(2): 157–162.

8. Borckardt, J. J., Reeves, S. T., et al. (2011). Fast left prefrontal rTMS acutely suppresses analgesic effects of perceived controllability on the emotional component of pain experience. *Pain, 152*(1): 182–187.

9. Schwartz, et al. (2002). Maximizing versus satisficing.

10. Bystritsky, A. (2006). Treatment-resistant anxiety disorders. *Molecular Psychiatry, 11*(9): 805–814.

11. Harris, S., Sheth, S. A., & Cohen, M. S. (2008). Functional neuroimaging of belief, disbelief, and uncertainty. *Annals of Neurology, 63*(2): 141–147.

12. Cabib, S., & Puglisi-Allegra, S. (2012). The mesoaccumbens dopamine in coping with stress. *Neuroscience & Biobehavioral Reviews, 36*(1): 79–89.

13. Lieberman, M. D., Eisenberger, N. I., et al. (2007). Putting feelings into words: Affect labeling disrupts amygdala activity in response to affective stimuli. *Psychological Science, 18*(5): 421–428.

14. Hoehn-Saric, R., Lee, J. S., et al. (2005). Effect of worry on regional cerebral blood flow in nonanxious subjects. *Psychiatry Research, 140*(3): 259–269.

15. Farb, N. A., Segal, Z. V., et al. (2007). Attending to the present: Mindfulness meditation reveals distinct neural modes of self-reference. *Social Cognitive and Affective Neuroscience, 2*(4): 313–322.

16. Holzel, B. K., Hoge, E. A., et al. (2013). Neural mechanisms of symptom improvements in generalized anxiety disorder following mindfulness training. *NeuroImage Clinical, 2*: 448–458.

Chapter 3

1. Vuilleumier, P. (2005). How brains beware: Neural mechanisms of emotional attention. *Trends in Cognitive Sciences, 9*(12): 585–594.

2. Mohanty, A., & Sussman, T. J. (2013). Top-down modulation of attention by emotion. *Frontiers in Human Neuroscience, 7*: 102.

3. Sander, D., Grandjean, D., et al. (2005). Emotion and attention interactions in social cognition: Brain regions involved in processing anger prosody. *Neuroimage, 28*(4): 848–858.

4. Rainville, P., Duncan, G. H., et al. (1997). Pain affect encoded in human anterior cingulate but not somatosensory cortex. *Science, 277*(5328): 968–971.

5. Carter, C. S., Braver, T. S., et al. (1998). Anterior cingulate cortex, error detection, and the online monitoring of performance. *Science, 280*(5364): 747–749.

6. Lawrence, N. S., Jollant, F., et al. (2009). Distinct roles of prefrontal cortical subregions in the Iowa Gambling Task. *Cerebral Cortex, 19*(5): 1134–1143.

7. Maniglio, R., Gusciglio, F., et al. (2014). Biased processing of neutral facial expressions is associated with depressive symptoms and suicide ideation in individuals at risk for major depression due to affective temperaments. *Comprehensive Psychiatry, 55*(3): 518–525.

8. Siegle, G. J., Steinhauer, S. R., et al. (2002). Can't shake that feeling: Event-related fMRI assessment of sustained amygdala activity in response to emotional information in depressed individuals. *Biological Psychiatry, 51*(9): 693–707.

9. Baumeister, R. F., Bratslavsky, E., et al. (2001). Bad is stronger than good. *Review of General Psychology, 5*(4): 323–370.

10. Waugh, C. E., Hamilton, J. P., & Gotlib, I. H. (2010). The neural temporal dynamics of the intensity of emotional experience. *Neuroimage, 49*(2): 1699–1707.

11. Maratos, E. J., Dolan, R. J., et al. (2001). Neural activity associated with episodic memory for emotional context. *Neuropsychologia, 39*(9): 910–920.

12. Fredrickson, B. L., & Losada, M. F. (2005). Positive affect and the complex dynamics of human flourishing. *American Psychologist, 60*(7): 678–686.

13. Dannlowski, U., Ohrmann, P., et al. (2007). Amygdala reactivity predicts automatic negative evaluations for facial emotions. *Psychiatry Research, 154*(1): 13–20.

14. Joormann, J., Talbot, L., & Gotlib, I. H. (2007). Biased processing of emotional information in girls at risk for depression. *Journal of Abnormal Psychology, 116*(1): 135–143.

15. Karg, K., Burmeister, M., et al. (2011). The serotonin transporter promoter variant (5-HTTLPR), stress, and depression meta-analysis revisited: Evidence of genetic moderation. *Archives of General Psychiatry, 68*(5): 444–454.

16. Perez-Edgar, K., Bar-Haim, Y., et al. (2010). Variations in the serotonin-transporter gene are associated with attention bias patterns to positive and negative emotion faces. *Biological Psychology, 83*(3): 269–271.

17. Sharot, T., Riccardi, A. M., et al. (2007). Neural mechanisms mediating optimism bias. *Nature, 450*(7166): 102–105.

18. Korb, A. S., Hunter, A. M., et al. (2009). Rostral anterior cingulate cortex theta current density and response to antidepressants and placebo in major depression. *Clinical Neurophysiology, 120*(7): 1313–1319.

19. Pezawas, L., Meyer-Lindenberg, A., et al. (2005). 5-HTTLPR polymorphism impacts human cingulate-amygdala interactions: A

genetic susceptibility mechanism for depression. *Nature Neuroscience, 8*(6): 828–834.

20. Hariri, A. R., Drabant, E. M., et al. (2005). A susceptibility gene for affective disorders and the response of the human amygdala. *Archives of General Psychiatry, 62*(2): 146–152.

21. Pichon, S., Rieger, S. W., & Vuilleumier, P. (2012). Persistent affective biases in human amygdala response following implicit priming with negative emotion concepts. *Neuroimage, 62*(3): 1610–1621.

22. Koster, E. H., De Raedt, R., et al. (2005). Mood-congruent attentional bias in dysphoria: Maintained attention to and impaired disengagement from negative information. *Emotion, 5*(4): 446–455.

23. Gotlib, I. H., Krasnoperova, E., et al. (2004). Attentional biases for negative interpersonal stimuli in clinical depression. *Journal of Abnormal Psychology, 113*(1): 121–135.

24. Carter, et al. (1998). Anterior cingulate cortex.

25. Holzel, B. K., Hoge, E. A., et al. (2013). Neural mechanisms of symptom improvements in generalized anxiety disorder following mindfulness training. *NeuroImage Clinical, 2*: 448–458.

26. Kerns, J. G. (2006). Anterior cingulate and prefrontal cortex activity in an FMRI study of trial-to-trial adjustments on the Simon task. *Neuroimage, 33*(1): 399–405.

27. Herwig, U., Bruhl, A. B., et al. (2010). Neural correlates of "pessimistic" attitude in depression. *Psychological Medicine, 40*(5): 789–800.

28. Strunk, D. R., & Adler, A. D. (2009). Cognitive biases in three prediction tasks: A test of the cognitive model of depression. *Behaviour Research and Therapy, 47*(1): 34–40.

29. Rainville, et al. (1997). Pain affect encoded in human anterior cingulate.

30. Strigo, I. A., Simmons, A. N., et al. (2008). Association of major depressive disorder with altered functional brain response during anticipation and processing of heat pain. *Archives of General Psychiatry, 65*(11): 1275–1284.

31. Phelps, E. A. (2004). Human emotion and memory: Interactions of the amygdala and hippocampal complex. *Current Opinion in Neurobiology, 14*(2): 198–202.

32. Macoveanu, J., Knorr, U., et al. (2013). Altered reward processing in the orbitofrontal cortex and hippocampus in healthy first-degree relatives of patients with depression. *Psychological Medicine*: 1–13.

33. Harmer, C. J., Shelley, N. C., et al. (2004). Increased positive versus negative affective perception and memory in healthy volunteers following selective serotonin and norepinephrine reuptake inhibition. *American Journal of Psychiatry, 161*(7): 1256–1263.

34. Morgan, V., Pickens, D., et al. (2005). Amitriptyline reduces rectal pain related activation of the anterior cingulate cortex in patients with irritable bowel syndrome. *Gut, 54*(5): 601–607.

35. Sharot, et al. (2007). Neural mechanism mediating optimism bias.

36. Herwig, U., Kaffenberger, T., et al. (2007). Neural correlates of a "pessimistic" attitude when anticipating events of unknown emotional valence. *Neuroimage, 34*(2): 848–858.

Chapter 4

1. Moore, C. M., Christensen, J. D., et al. (1997). Lower levels of nucleoside triphosphate in the basal ganglia of depressed subjects: A phosphorous-31 magnetic resonance spectroscopy study. *American Journal of Psychiatry, 154*(1): 116–118.

2. Scott, D. J., Heitzeg, M. M., et al. (2006). Variations in the human pain stress experience mediated by ventral and dorsal basal ganglia dopamine activity. *Journal of Neuroscience, 26*(42): 10789–10795.

3. Schwabe, L., & Wolf, O. T. (2009). Stress prompts habit behavior in humans. *Journal of Neuroscience, 29*(22): 7191–7198.

Chapter 5

1. Akbaraly, T., Brunner, E. J., et al. (2009). Dietary pattern and depressive symptoms in middle age. *British Journal of Psychiatry, 195*(5): 408–413.

2. Colcombe, S., & Kramer, A. F. (2003). Fitness effects on the cognitive function of older adults: A meta-analytic study. *Psychological Science, 14*(2): 125–130.

3. Reid, K. J., Baron, K. G., et al. (2010). Aerobic exercise improves self-reported sleep and quality of life in older adults with insomnia. *Sleep Medicine, 11*(9): 934–940.

4. Petruzzello, S. J., Landers, D. M., et al. (1991). A meta-analysis on the anxiety-reducing effects of acute and chronic exercise. Outcomes and mechanisms. *Sports Medicine, 11*(3): 143–182.

5. Blumenthal, J. A., Fredrikson, M., et al. (1990). Aerobic exercise reduces levels of cardiovascular and sympathoadrenal responses to mental stress in subjects without prior evidence of myocardial ischemia. *American Journal of Cardiology, 65*(1): 93–98.

6. Cotman, C. W., & Berchtold, N. C. (2002). Exercise: A behavioral intervention to enhance brain health and plasticity. *Trends in Neurosciences, 25*(6): 295–301.

7. Leasure, J. L., & Jones, M. (2008). Forced and voluntary exercise differentially affect brain and behavior. *Neuroscience, 156*(3): 456–465.

8. Pretty, J., Peacock, J., et al. (2005). The mental and physical health outcomes of green exercise. *International Journal of Environmental Health Research, 15*(5): 319–337.

9. Kaplan, R. (2001). The nature of the view from home: Psychological benefits. *Environment and Behavior, 33*: 507–542.

10. Rovio, S., Spulber, G., et al. (2010). The effect of midlife physical activity on structural brain changes in the elderly. *Neurobiology of Aging, 31*(11): 1927–1936.

11. Balu, D. T., Hoshaw, B. A., et al. (2008). Differential regulation of central BDNF protein levels by antidepressant and non-antidepressant drug treatments. *Brain Research, 1211*: 37–43.

12. Jacobs, B. L., & Fornal, C. A. (1999). Activity of serotonergic neurons in behaving animals. *Neuropsychopharmacology, 21*(2 Suppl): 9S–15S.

13. Rueter, L. E., & Jacobs, B. L. (1996). A microdialysis examination of serotonin release in the rat forebrain induced by behavioral/environmental manipulations. *Brain Research, 739*(1–2): 57–69.

14. Mattson, M. P., Maudsley, S., & Martin, B. (2004). BDNF and 5-HT: A dynamic duo in age-related neuronal plasticity and neurodegenerative disorders. *Trends in Neurosciences, 27*(10): 589–594.

15. Winter, B., Breitenstein, C., et al. (2007). High impact running improves learning. *Neurobiology of Learning and Memory, 87*(4): 597–609.

16. Winter, et al. (2007). High impact running.

17. Janse Van Rensburg, K., Taylor, A., et al. (2009). Acute exercise modulates cigarette cravings and brain activation in response to smoking-related images: An fMRI study. *Psychopharmacology (Berl), 203*(3): 589–598.

18. Boecker, H., Sprenger, T., et al. (2008). The runner's high: Opioidergic mechanisms in the human brain. *Cerebral Cortex, 18*(11): 2523–2531.

19. Goldfarb, A. H., Hatfield, B. D., et al. (1990). Plasma beta-endorphin concentration: Response to intensity and duration of exercise. *Medicine & Science in Sports & Exercise, 22*(2): 241–244.

20. Sparling, P. B., Giuffrida, A., et al. (2003). Exercise activates the endocannabinoid system. *Neuroreport, 14*(17): 2209–2211.

21. Nabkasorn, C., Miyai, N., et al. (2006). Effects of physical exercise on depression, neuroendocrine stress hormones and physiological fitness in adolescent females with depressive symptoms. *European Journal of Public Health, 16*(2): 179–184.

22. Fumoto, M., Oshima, T., et al. (2010). Ventral prefrontal cortex and serotonergic system activation during pedaling exercise induces negative mood improvement and increased alpha band in EEG. *Behavioural Brain Research, 213*(1): 1–9.

23. Reid, et al. (2010). Aerobic exercise improves self-reported sleep.

24. Pillai, V., Kalmbach, D. A., & Ciesla, J. A. (2011). A meta-analysis of electroencephalographic sleep in depression: Evidence for genetic biomarkers. *Biological Psychiatry, 70*(10): 912–919.

25. Sharpley, A. L., & Cowen, P. J. (1995). Effect of pharmacologic treatments on the sleep of depressed patients. *Biological Psychiatry, 37*(2): 85–98.

Chapter 6

1. Schwartz, B., Ward, A., et al. (2002). Maximizing versus satisficing: Happiness is a matter of choice. *Journal of Personality and Social Psychology, 83*(5): 1178–1197.

2. Venkatraman, V., Payne, J. W., et al. (2009). Separate neural mechanisms underlie choices and strategic preferences in risky decision making. *Neuron, 62*(4): 593–602.

3. de Wit, S., Corlett, P. R., et al. (2009). Differential engagement of the ventromedial prefrontal cortex by goal-directed and habitual behavior toward food pictures in humans. *Journal of Neuroscience, 29*(36): 11330–11338.

4. Gazzaley, A., Cooney, J. W., et al. (2005). Top-down enhancement and suppression of the magnitude and speed of neural activity. *Journal of Cognitive Neuroscience, 17*(3): 507–517.

5. Creswell, J. D., Welch, W. T., et al. (2005). Affirmation of personal values buffers neuroendocrine and psychological stress responses. *Psychological Science, 16*(11): 846–851.

6. Wykowska, A., & Schubo, A. (2012). Action intentions modulate allocation of visual attention: Electrophysiological evidence. *Frontiers in Psychology, 3*: 379.

7. Hemby, S. E., Co, C., et al. (1997). Differences in extracellular dopamine concentrations in the nucleus accumbens during response-dependent and response-independent cocaine administration in the rat. *Psychopharmacology (Berl), 133*(1): 7–16.

8. Luce, M. F., Bettman, J. R., & Payne, J. W. (1997). Choice processing in emotionally difficult decisions. *Journal of Experimental Psychology, Learning, Memory, and Cognition, 23*(2): 384–405.

9. Gallagher, K. M., & Updegraff, J. A. (2012). Health message framing effects on attitudes, intentions, and behavior: A meta-analytic review. *Annals of Behavioral Medicine, 43*(1): 101–116.

10. Studer, B., Apergis-Schoute, A. M., et al. (2012). What are the Odds? The neural correlates of active choice during gambling. *Frontiers in Neuroscience, 6*: 46.

11. Rao, H., Korczykowski, M., et al. (2008). Neural correlates of voluntary and involuntary risk taking in the human brain: An fMRI study

of the Balloon Analog Risk Task (BART). *Neuroimage, 42*(2): 902–910.

12. Lieberman, M. D., Ochsner, K. N., et al. (2001). Do amnesics exhibit cognitive dissonance reduction? The role of explicit memory and attention in attitude change. *Psychological Science, 12*(2): 135–140.

13. MacLeod, A. K., Coates, E., & Hetherton, J. (2008). Increasing well-being through teaching goal-setting and planning skills: Results of a brief intervention. *Journal of Happiness Studies 9*: 185–196.

14. Dickson, J. M., & Moberly, N. J. (2013). Reduced specificity of personal goals and explanations for goal attainment in major depression. *PLoS One, 8*(5): e64512.

15. Hadley, S. A., & MacLeod, A. K. (2010). Conditional goal-setting, personal goals and hopelessness about the future. *Cognition & Emotion, 24*(7): 1191–1198.

16. Draganski, B., Kherif, F., et al. (2008). Evidence for segregated and integrative connectivity patterns in the human basal ganglia. *Journal of Neuroscience, 28*(28): 7143–7152.

17. Weiss, J. M., Goodman, P. A., et al. (1981). Behavioral depression produced by an uncontrollable stressor: Relationship to norepinephrine, dopamine, and serotonin levels in various regions of rat brain. *Brain Research Reviews, 3*(2): 167–205.

18. Wiech, K., Kalisch, R., et al. (2006). Anterolateral prefrontal cortex mediates the analgesic effect of expected and perceived control over pain. *Journal of Neuroscience, 26*(44): 11501–11509.

19. Greenwood, B. N., Foley, T. E., et al. (2003). Freewheel running prevents learned helplessness/behavioral depression: Role of dorsal raphe serotonergic neurons. *Journal of Neuroscience, 23*(7): 2889–2898.

20. Yanagita, S., Amemiya, S., et al. (2007). Effects of spontaneous and forced running on activation of hypothalamic corticotropin-releasing hormone neurons in rats. *Life Sciences, 80*(4): 356–363.

21. Thrift, M., Ulloa-Heath, J., et al. (2012). Career interventions and the career thoughts of Pacific Island College students. *Journal of Counseling & Development, 90*(2): 169–176.

22. Frost, R. O., & Shows, D. L. (1993). The nature and measurement of compulsive indecisiveness. *Behaviour Research and Therapy, 31*(7): 683–692.

Chapter 7

1. Nofzinger, E. A., Nissen, C., et al. (2006). Regional cerebral metabolic correlates of WASO during NREM sleep in insomnia. *Journal of Clinical Sleep Medicine, 2*(3): 316–322.

2. Pillai, V., Kalmbach, D. A., & Ciesla, J. A. (2011). A meta-analysis of electroencephalographic sleep in depression: Evidence for genetic biomarkers. *Biological Psychiatry, 70*(10): 912–919.

3. Sharpley, A. L., & Cowen, P. J. (1995). Effect of pharmacologic treatments on the sleep of depressed patients. *Biological Psychiatry, 37*(2): 85–98.

4. Irwin, M., McClintick, J., et al. (1996). Partial night sleep deprivation reduces natural killer and cellular immune responses in humans. *FASEB Journal, 10*(5): 643–653.

5. Brower, K. J., & Perron, B. E. (2010). Sleep disturbance as a universal risk factor for relapse in addictions to psychoactive substances. *Medical Hypotheses, 74*(5): 928–933.

6. Harrison, Y., & Horne, J. A. (1999). One night of sleep loss impairs innovative thinking and flexible decision making. *Organizational Behavior and Human Decision Processes, 78*(2): 128–145.

7. Altena, E., Van Der Werf, Y. D., et al. (2008). Sleep loss affects vigilance: Effects of chronic insomnia and sleep therapy. *Journal of Sleep Research, 17*(3): 335–343.

8. Altena, E., Van Der Werf, Y. D., et al. (2008). Prefrontal hypoactivation and recovery in insomnia. *Sleep, 31*(9): 1271–1276.

9. Nofzinger, et al. (2006). Regional cerebral metabolic correlates.

10. Brown, F. C., Buboltz, W. C., Jr., & Soper, B. (2002). Relationship of sleep hygiene awareness, sleep hygiene practices, and sleep quality in university students. *Behavioral Medicine, 28*(1): 33–38.

11. Sivertsen, B., Salo, P., et al. (2012). The bidirectional association between depression and insomnia: The HUNT study. *Psychosomatic Medicine, 74*(7): 758–765.

12. Wierzynski, C. M., Lubenov, E. V., et al. (2009). State-dependent spike-timing relationships between hippocampal and prefrontal circuits during sleep. *Neuron, 61*(4): 587–596.

13. Yoo, S. S., Hu, P. T., et al. (2007). A deficit in the ability to form new human memories without sleep. *Nature Neuroscience, 10*(3): 385–392.

14. Wilhelm, I., Diekelmann, S., et al. (2011). Sleep selectively enhances memory expected to be of future relevance. *Journal of Neuroscience, 31*(5): 1563–1569.

15. Fischer, S., & Born, J. (2009). Anticipated reward enhances offline learning during sleep. *Journal of Experimental Psychology, Learning, Memory, and Cognition, 35*(6): 1586–1593.

16. Van Der Werf, Y. D., Altena, E., et al. (2009). Sleep benefits subsequent hippocampal functioning. *Nature Neuroscience, 12*(2): 122–123.

17. Mishima, K., Okawa, M., et al. (2001). Diminished melatonin secretion in the elderly caused by insufficient environmental illumination. *Journal of Clinical Endocrinology and Metabolism, 86*(1): 129–134.

18. Lambert, G. W., Reid, C., et al. (2002). Effect of sunlight and season on serotonin turnover in the brain. *Lancet, 360*(9348): 1840–1842.

19. Walch, J. M., Rabin, B. S., et al. (2005). The effect of sunlight on postoperative analgesic medication use: A prospective study of patients undergoing spinal surgery. *Psychosomatic Medicine, 67*(1): 156–163.

20. Mishima, et al. (2001). Diminished melatonin secretion in the elderly.

21. Babson, K. A., Trainor, C. D., et al. (2010). A test of the effects of acute sleep deprivation on general and specific self-reported anxiety and depressive symptoms: An experimental extension. *Journal of Behavior Therapy and Experimental Psychiatry, 41*(3): 297–303.

22. Monti, J. M., & Jantos, H. (2008). The roles of dopamine and serotonin, and of their receptors, in regulating sleep and waking. *Progress in Brain Research, 172*: 625–646.

23. Dominguez-Lopez, S., Mahar, I., et al. (2012). Short-term effects of melatonin and pinealectomy on serotonergic neuronal activity across the light-dark cycle. *Journal of Psychopharmacology, 26*(6): 830–844.

24. Pontes, A. L. B., Engelberth, R. C. J. G., et al. (2010). Serotonin and circadian rhythms. *Psychology and Neuroscience, 3*: 217–228.

25. Murray, G., Nicholas, C. L., et al. (2009). Nature's clocks and human mood: The circadian system modulates reward motivation. *Emotion, 9*(5): 705–716.

26. Basta, M., Chrousos, G. P., et al. (2007). Chronic insomnia and stress system. *Sleep Medicine Clinics*, 2(2): 279–291.

27. Kim, Y., Chen, L., et al. (2013). Sleep allostasis in chronic sleep restriction: The role of the norepinephrine system. *Brain Research*, 1531: 9–16.

28. Monti & Jantos. (2008). The roles of dopamine and serotonin.

29. Finan, P. H., & Smith, M. T. (2013). The comorbidity of insomnia, chronic pain, and depression: Dopamine as a putative mechanism. *Sleep Medicine Reviews*, 17(3): 173–183.

30. McClung, C. A. (2007). Circadian rhythms, the mesolimbic dopaminergic circuit, and drug addiction. *Scientific World Journal*, 7: 194–202.

31. Finan & Smith. (2013). The comorbidity of insomnia, chronic pain, and depression.

32. Babson, et al. (2010). A test of the effect of acute sleep deprivation.

33. O'Brien, E. M., Waxenberg, L. B., et al. (2010). Negative mood mediates the effect of poor sleep on pain among chronic pain patients. *Clinical Journal of Pain*, 26(4): 310–319.

34. Smith, M. T., Edwards, R. R., et al. (2007). The effects of sleep deprivation on pain inhibition and spontaneous pain in women. *Sleep*, 30(4): 494–505.

35. Campbell, C. M., Bounds, S. C., et al. (2013). Individual variation in sleep quality and duration is related to cerebral mu opioid receptor binding potential during tonic laboratory pain in healthy subjects. *Pain Medicine*, 14(12): 1882–1892.

36. Xie, L., Kang, H., et al. (2013). Sleep drives metabolite clearance from the adult brain. *Science*, 342(6156): 373–377.

37. Brown, Buboltz, & Soper. (2002). Relationship of sleep hygiene awareness.

38. Roehrs, T., & Roth, T. (2001). Sleep, sleepiness, sleep disorders and alcohol use and abuse. *Sleep Medicine Reviews*, 5(4): 287–297.

39. Irwin, M., Miller, C., et al. (2000). Polysomnographic and spectral sleep EEG in primary alcoholics: An interaction between alcohol dependence and African-American ethnicity. *Alcoholism Clinical and Experimental Research*, 24(9): 1376–1384.

40. Reid, K. J., Baron, K. G., et al. (2010). Aerobic exercise improves self-reported sleep and quality of life in older adults with insomnia. *Sleep Medicine, 11*(9): 934–940.

41. Miro, E., Lupianez, J., et al. (2011). Cognitive-behavioral therapy for insomnia improves attentional function in fibromyalgia syndrome: A pilot, randomized controlled trial. *Journal of Health Psychology, 16*(5): 770–782.

42. Dirksen, S. R., & Epstein, D. R. (2008). Efficacy of an insomnia intervention on fatigue, mood and quality of life in breast cancer survivors. *Journal of Advanced Nursing, 61*(6): 664–675.

Chapter 8

1. Armitage, C. J., Harris, P. R., et al. (2008). Self-affirmation increases acceptance of health-risk information among UK adult smokers with low socioeconomic status. *Psychology of Addictive Behaviors, 22*(1): 88–95.

2. Epton, T., & Harris, P. R. (2008). Self-affirmation promotes health behavior change. *Health Psychology, 27*(6): 746–752.

3. Perreau-Linck, E., Beauregard, M., et al. (2007). In vivo measurements of brain trapping of C-labelled alpha-methyl-L-tryptophan during acute changes in mood states. *Journal of Psychiatry & Neuroscience, 32*(6): 430–434.

4. Ochsner, K. N., Ray, R. D., et al. (2004). For better or for worse: Neural systems supporting the cognitive down- and up-regulation of negative emotion. *Neuroimage, 23*(2): 483–499.

5. Soares, J. M., Sampaio, A., et al. (2012). Stress-induced changes in human decision-making are reversible. *Translational Psychiatry, 2*: e131.

6. Schwabe, L., & Wolf, O. T. (2009). Stress prompts habit behavior in humans. *Journal of Neuroscience, 29*(22): 7191–7198.

7. Norcross, J. C., Mrykalo, M. S., & Blagys, M. D. (2002). Auld lang syne: Success predictors, change processes, and self-reported outcomes of New Year's resolvers and nonresolvers. *Journal of Clinical Psychology, 58*(4): 397–405.

8. Ayduk, O., Mendoza-Denton, R., et al. (2000). Regulating the interpersonal self: Strategic self-regulation for coping with rejection sensitivity. *Journal of Personality and Social Psychology, 79*(5): 776–792.

9. Casey, B. J., Somerville, L. H., et al. (2011). Behavioral and neural correlates of delay of gratification 40 years later. *Proceedings of the National Academy of Sciences USA, 108*(36): 14998–15003.

10. Young, S. N. (2007). How to increase serotonin in the human brain without drugs. *Journal of Psychiatry & Neuroscience, 32*(6): 394–399.

11. Field, T., Hernandez-Reif, M., et al. (2005). Cortisol decreases and serotonin and dopamine increase following massage therapy. *International Journal of Neuroscience, 115*(10): 1397–1413.

12. Perreau-Linck, et al. (2007). In vivo measurements.

13. Goto, Y., & Grace, A. A. (2005). Dopaminergic modulation of limbic and cortical drive of nucleus accumbens in goal-directed behavior. *Nature Neuroscience, 8*(6): 805–812.

14. Feldstein Ewing, S. W., Filbey, F. M., et al. (2011). How psychosocial alcohol interventions work: A preliminary look at what FMRI can tell us. *Alcoholism Clinical and Experimental Research, 35*(4): 643–651.

15. Lieberman, M. D., Eisenberger, N. I., et al. (2007). Putting feelings into words: Affect labeling disrupts amygdala activity in response to affective stimuli. *Psychological Science, 18*(5): 421–428.

Chapter 9

1. Shapiro, D., Cook, I. A., et al. (2007). Yoga as a complementary treatment of depression: Effects of traits and moods on treatment outcome. *Evidence-Based Complementary and Alternative Medicine, 4*(4): 493–502.

2. Leino, P., & Magni, G. (1993). Depressive and distress symptoms as predictors of low back pain, neck-shoulder pain, and other musculoskeletal morbidity: A 10-year follow-up of metal industry employees. *Pain, 53*(1): 89–94.

3. Carney, R. M., Blumenthal, J. A., et al. (2001). Depression, heart rate variability, and acute myocardial infarction. *Circulation, 104*(17): 2024–2028.

4. Nakahara, H., Furuya, S., et al. (2009). Emotion-related changes in heart rate and its variability during performance and perception of music. *Annals of the New York Academy of Sciences, 1169*: 359–362.

5. Brown, S., Martinez, M. J., & Parsons, L. M. (2004). Passive music listening spontaneously engages limbic and paralimbic systems. *Neuroreport, 15*(13): 2033–2037.

6. Sutoo, D., & Akiyama, K. (2004). Music improves dopaminergic neurotransmission: Demonstration based on the effect of music on blood pressure regulation. *Brain Research, 1016*(2): 255–262.

7. Strack, F., Martin, L. L., & Stepper, S. (1988). Inhibiting and facilitating conditions of the human smile: A nonobtrusive test of the facial feedback hypothesis. *Journal of Personality and Social Psychology, 54*(5): 768–777.

8. Dimberg, U., & Soderkvist, S. (2011). The voluntary facial action technique: A method to test the facial feedback hypothesis. *Journal of Nonverbal Behavior, 35*: 17–33.

9. Mora-Ripoll, R. (2010). The therapeutic value of laughter in medicine. *Alternative Therapies, Health, and Medicine, 16*(6): 56–64.

10. Fischer, J., Fischer, P., et al. (2011). Empower my decisions: The effects of power gestures on confirmatory information processing. *Journal of Experimental Social Psychology, 47*: 1146–1154.

11. Brinol, P., Petty, R. E., & Wagner, B. (2009). Body posture effects on self-evaluation: A self-validation approach. *European Journal of Social Psychology, 39*: 1053–1064.

12. Riskind, J. H., & Gotay, C. C. (1982). Physical posture: Could it have regulatory or feedback effects on motivation and emotion? *Motivation and Emotion, 6*(3): 273–298.

13. Peper, E., & Lin, I. (2012). Increase or decrease depression: How body postures influence your energy level. *Biofeedback, 40*(3): 125–130.

14. Carney, D. R., Cuddy, A. J., & Yap, A. J. (2010). Power posing: Brief nonverbal displays affect neuroendocrine levels and risk tolerance. *Psychological Science, 21*(10): 1363–1368.

15. Larsen, R. J., Kasimatis, M., & Frey, K. (1992). Facilitating the furrowed brow: An unobtrusive test of the facial feedback hypothesis applied to unpleasant affect. *Cognition & Emotion, 6*(5): 321–338.

16. Duclos, S. E., & Laird, J. D. (2001). The deliberate control of emotional experience through control of expressions. *Cognition & Emotion, 15*(1): 27–56.

17. Lewis, M. B., & Bowler, P. J. (2009). Botulinum toxin cosmetic therapy correlates with a more positive mood. *Journal of Cosmetic Dermatology, 8*(1): 24–26.

18. Kunik, M. E., Roundy, K., et al. (2005). Surprisingly high prevalence of anxiety and depression in chronic breathing disorders. *Chest, 127*(4): 1205–1211.

19. Kjellgren, A., Bood, S. A., et al. (2007). Wellness through a comprehensive yogic breathing program: A controlled pilot trial. *BMC Complementary and Alternative Medicine, 7*: 43.

20. McPartland, J. M. (2008). Expression of the endocannabinoid system in fibroblasts and myofascial tissues. *Journal of Bodywork and Movement Therapies, 12*(2): 169–182.

21. Nerbass, F. B., Feltrim, M. I., et al. (2010). Effects of massage therapy on sleep quality after coronary artery bypass graft surgery. *Clinics (Sao Paulo), 65*(11): 1105–1110.

22. Field, T., Hernandez-Reif, M., et al. (2005). Cortisol decreases and serotonin and dopamine increase following massage therapy. *International Journal of Neuroscience, 115*(10): 1397–1413.

Chapter 10

1. Watkins, P. C., Woodward, K., et al. (2003). Gratitude and happiness: Development of a measure of gratitude, and relationship with subjective well-being. *Social Behavior and Personality, 31*(5): 431–452.

2. Kleiman, E. M., Adams, L. M., et al. (2013). Grateful individuals are not suicidal: Buffering risks associated with hopelessness and depressive symptoms. *Personality and Individual Differences, 55*(5): 595–599.

3. Froh, J. J., Yurkewicz, C., & Kashdan, T. B. (2009). Gratitude and subjective well-being in early adolescence: Examining gender differences. *Journal of Adolescence, 32*(3): 633–650.

4. Ng, M. Y., & Wong, W. S. (2013). The differential effects of gratitude and sleep on psychological distress in patients with chronic pain. *Journal of Health Psychology, 18*(2): 263–271.

5. Hill, P. L., Allemand, M., & Roberts, B. W. (2013). Examining the pathways between gratitude and self-rated physical health across adulthood. *Personality and Individual Differences, 54*(1): 92–96.

6. Emmons, R. A., & McCullough, M. E. (2003). Counting blessings versus burdens: An experimental investigation of gratitude and subjective well-being in daily life. *Journal of Personality and Social Psychology, 84*(2): 377–389.

7. Wood, A. M., Maltby, J., et al. (2008). The role of gratitude in the development of social support, stress, and depression: Two longitudinal studies. *Journal of Research in Personality, 42*: 854–871.

8. Zahn, R., Moll, J., et al. (2009). The neural basis of human social values: Evidence from functional MRI. *Cerebral Cortex, 19*(2): 276–283.

9. Perreau-Linck, E., Beauregard, M., et al. (2007). In vivo measurements of brain trapping of C-labelled alpha-methyl-L-tryptophan during acute changes in mood states. *Journal of Psychiatry & Neuroscience, 32*(6): 430–434.

10. Digdon, N., & Koble, A. (2011). Effects of constructive worry, imagery distraction, and gratitude interventions on sleep quality: A pilot trial. *Applied Psychology: Health and Well-being, 3*(2): 193–206.

11. Ng & Wong. (2013). The differential effects of gratitude and sleep.

12. Sharot, T., Riccardi, A. M., et al. (2007). Neural mechanisms mediating optimism bias. *Nature, 450*(7166): 102–105.

13. Immordino-Yang, M. H., McColl, A., et al. (2009). Neural correlates of admiration and compassion. *Proceedings of the National Academy of Sciences USA, 106*(19): 8021–8026.

14. Bartolo, A., Benuzzi, F., et al. (2006). Humor comprehension and appreciation: An FMRI study. *Journal of Cognitive Neuroscience, 18*(11): 1789–1798.

15. Mobbs, D., Greicius, M. D., et al. (2003). Humor modulates the mesolimbic reward centers. *Neuron, 40*(5): 1041–1048.

16. Roth, L., Kaffenberger, T., et al. (2014). Brain activation associated with pride and shame. *Neuropsychobiology, 69*(2): 95–106.

17. Emmons & McCullough. (2003). Counting blessings versus burdens.

18. Lambert, N. M., Fincham, F. D., et al. (2009). More gratitude, less materialism: The mediating role of life satisfaction. *Journal of Positive Psychology, 4*(1): 32–42.

19. Takeuchi, H., Taki, Y., et al. (2011). Regional gray matter density associated with emotional intelligence: Evidence from voxel-based morphometry. *Human Brain Mapping, 32*(9): 1497–1510.

Chapter 11

1. Eisenberger, N. I., Jarcho, J. M., et al. (2006). An experimental study of shared sensitivity to physical pain and social rejection. *Pain, 126* (1–3): 132–138.

2. Onoda, K., Okamoto, Y., et al. (2010). Does low self-esteem enhance social pain? The relationship between trait self-esteem and anterior cingulate cortex activation induced by ostracism. *Social Cognitive and Affective Neuroscience, 5*(4): 385–391.

3. Tops, M., Riese, H., et al. (2008). Rejection sensitivity relates to hypo-cortisolism and depressed mood state in young women. *Psychoneuroendocrinology, 33*(5): 551–559.

4. Meynen, G., Unmehopa, U. A., et al. (2007). Hypothalamic oxytocin mRNA expression and melancholic depression. *Molecular Psychiatry, 12*(2): 118–119.

5. Cyranowski, J. M., Hofkens, T. L., et al. (2008). Evidence of dysregu-lated peripheral oxytocin release among depressed women. *Psychosomatic Medicine, 70*(9): 967–975.

6. Jokinen, J., Chatzittofis, A., et al. (2012). Low CSF oxytocin reflects high intent in suicide attempters. *Psychoneuroendocrinology, 37*(4): 482–490.

7. Heim, C., Young, L. J., et al. (2009). Lower CSF oxytocin concentra-tions in women with a history of childhood abuse. *Molecular Psychiatry, 14*(10): 954–958.

8. Thompson, R. J., Parker, K. J., et al. (2011). Oxytocin receptor gene polymorphism (rs2254298) interacts with familial risk for psychopathology to predict symptoms of depression and anxiety in adolescent girls. *Psychoneuroendocrinology, 36*(1): 144–147.

9. Costa, B., Pini, S., et al. (2009). Oxytocin receptor polymorphisms and adult attachment style in patients with depression. *Psychoneuroendocrinology, 34*(10): 1506–1514.

10. Bell, C. J., Nicholson, H., et al. (2006). Plasma oxytocin levels in depression and their correlation with the temperament dimension of reward dependence. *Journal of Psychopharmacology, 20*(5): 656–660.

11. Norman, G. J., Karelina, K., et al. (2010). Social interaction prevents the development of depressive-like behavior post nerve injury in mice: A potential role for oxytocin. *Psychosomatic Medicine, 72*(6): 519–526.

12. Brown, J. L., Sheffield, D., et al. (2003). Social support and experimental pain. *Psychosomatic Medicine, 65*(2): 276–283.

13. Montoya, P., Larbig, W., et al. (2004). Influence of social support and emotional context on pain processing and magnetic brain responses in fibromyalgia. *Arthritis and Rheumatology, 50*(12): 4035–4044.

14. Master, S. L., Eisenberger, N. I., et al. (2009). A picture's worth: Partner photographs reduce experimentally induced pain. *Psychological Science, 20*(11): 1316–1318.

15. Borsook, T. K., & MacDonald, G. (2010). Mildly negative social encounters reduce physical pain sensitivity. *Pain, 151*(2): 372–377.

16. Coan, J. A., Schaefer, H. S., & Davidson, R. J. (2006). Lending a hand: Social regulation of the neural response to threat. *Psychological Science, 17*(12): 1032–1039.

17. Sayal, K., Checkley, S., et al. (2002). Effects of social support during weekend leave on cortisol and depression ratings: A pilot study. *Journal of Affective Disorders, 71*(1–3): 153–157.

18. Joseph, N. T., Myers, H. F., et al. (2011). Support and undermining in interpersonal relationships are associated with symptom improvement in a trial of antidepressant medication. *Psychiatry, 74*(3): 240–254.

19. Epley, N., Schroeder, J., & Waytz, A. (2013). Motivated mind perception: Treating pets as people and people as animals. In S. J. Gervais

(Ed.), *Objectification and (De)Humanization* (pp. 127–152). New York: Springer.

20. Yoshida, M., Takayanagi, Y., et al. (2009). Evidence that oxytocin exerts anxiolytic effects via oxytocin receptor expressed in serotonergic neurons in mice. *Journal of Neuroscience, 29*(7): 2259–2271.

21. Heinrichs, M., Baumgartner, T., et al. (2003). Social support and oxytocin interact to suppress cortisol and subjective responses to psychosocial stress. *Biological Psychiatry, 54*(12): 1389–1398.

22. Domes, G., Heinrichs, M., et al. (2007). Oxytocin attenuates amygdala responses to emotional faces regardless of valence. *Biological Psychiatry, 62*(10): 1187–1190.

23. Riem, M. M., van IJzendoorn, M. H., et al. (2012). No laughing matter: Intranasal oxytocin administration changes functional brain connectivity during exposure to infant laughter. *Neuropsychopharmacology, 37*(5): 1257–1266.

24. Leuner, B., Caponiti, J. M., & Gould, E. (2012). Oxytocin stimulates adult neurogenesis even under conditions of stress and elevated glucocorticoids. *Hippocampus, 22*(4): 861–868.

25. Onoda, K., Okamoto, Y., et al. (2009). Decreased ventral anterior cingulate cortex activity is associated with reduced social pain during emotional support. *Social Neuroscience, 4*(5): 443–454.

26. Musick, M. A., & Wilson, J. (2003). Volunteering and depression: The role of psychological and social resources in different age groups. *Social Science & Medicine, 56*(2): 259–269.

27. Fowler, J. H., & Christakis, N. A. (2008). Dynamic spread of happiness in a large social network: Longitudinal analysis over 20 years in the Framingham Heart Study. *British Medical Journal, 337*: a2338.

28. Baskerville, T. A., & Douglas, A. J. (2010). Dopamine and oxytocin interactions underlying behaviors: Potential contributions to behavioral disorders. *CNS Neuroscience & Therapeutics, 16*(3): e92–123.

29. Sarnyai, Z., Vecsernyes, M., et al. (1992). Effects of cocaine on the contents of neurohypophyseal hormones in the plasma and in different brain structures in rats. *Neuropeptides, 23*(1): 27–31.

30. Carson, D. S., Hunt, G. E., et al. (2010). Systemically administered oxytocin decreases methamphetamine activation of the subthalamic

nucleus and accumbens core and stimulates oxytocinergic neurons in the hypothalamus. *Addiction Biology, 15*(4): 448–463.

31. Bowen, M. T., Carson, D. S., et al. (2011). Adolescent oxytocin exposure causes persistent reductions in anxiety and alcohol consumption and enhances sociability in rats. *PLoS One, 6*(11): e27237.

32. Uvnas-Moberg, K. (1998). Oxytocin may mediate the benefits of positive social interaction and emotions. *Psychoneuroendocrinology, 23*(8): 819–835.

33. Williams, L. E., & Bargh, J. A. (2008). Experiencing physical warmth promotes interpersonal warmth. *Science, 322*(5901): 606–607.

34. Lund, I., Ge, Y., et al. (2002). Repeated massage-like stimulation induces long-term effects on nociception: Contribution of oxytocinergic mechanisms. *European Journal of Neuroscience, 16*(2): 330–338.

35. Nerbass, F. B., Feltrim, M. I., et al. (2010). Effects of massage therapy on sleep quality after coronary artery bypass graft surgery. *Clinics (Sao Paulo), 65*(11): 1105–1110.

36. Field, T., Hernandez-Reif, M., et al. (2005). Cortisol decreases and serotonin and dopamine increase following massage therapy. *International Journal of Neuroscience, 115*(10): 1397–1413.

37. Eisenberger, N. I., Taylor, S. E., et al. (2007). Neural pathways link social support to attenuated neuroendocrine stress responses. *Neuroimage, 35*(4): 1601–1612.

38. Seltzer, L. J., Prososki, A. R., et al. (2012). Instant messages vs. speech: Hormones and why we still need to hear each other. *Evolution and Human Behavior, 33*(1): 42–45.

39. Suda, M., Takei, Y., et al. (2010). Frontopolar activation during face-to-face conversation: An in situ study using near-infrared spectroscopy. *Neuropsychologia, 48*(2): 441–447.

40. Seltzer, et al. (2012). Instant messages vs. speech.

41. Bernhardt, P. C., Dabbs, J. M., Jr., et al. (1998). Testosterone changes during vicarious experiences of winning and losing among fans at sporting events. *Physiology & Behavior, 65*(1): 59–62.

42. Karremans, J. C., Heslenfeld, D. J., et al. (2011). Secure attachment partners attenuate neural responses to social exclusion: An fMRI investigation. *International Journal of Psychophysiology, 81*(1): 44–50.

43. Motooka, M., Koike, H., et al. (2006). Effect of dog-walking on autonomic nervous activity in senior citizens. *Medical Journal of Australia, 184*(2): 60–63.

44. Nagasawa, M., Kikusui, T., et al. (2009). Dog's gaze at its owner increases owner's urinary oxytocin during social interaction. *Hormones and Behavior, 55*(3): 434–441.

45. Odendaal, J. S., & Meintjes, R. A. (2003). Neurophysiological correlates of affiliative behaviour between humans and dogs. *Veterinary Journal, 165*(3): 296–301.

46. Colombo, G., Buono, M. D., et al. (2006). Pet therapy and institutionalized elderly: A study on 144 cognitively unimpaired subjects. *Archives of Gerontology and Geriatrics, 42*(2): 207–216.

47. Eddy, J., Hart, L. A., & Boltz, R. P. (1988). The effects of service dogs on social acknowledgments of people in wheelchairs. *Journal of Psychology, 122*(1): 39–45.

48. Baskerville & Douglas. (2010). Dopamine and oxytocin interactions underlying behaviors.

49. Riem, M. M., Bakermans-Kranenburg, M. J., et al. (2011). Oxytocin modulates amygdala, insula, and inferior frontal gyrus responses to infant crying: A randomized controlled trial. *Biological Psychiatry, 70*(3): 291–297.

50. Bakermans-Kranenburg, M. J., van IJzendoorn, M. H., et al. (2012). Oxytocin decreases handgrip force in reaction to infant crying in females without harsh parenting experiences. *Social Cognitive and Affective Neuroscience, 7*(8): 951–957.

51. Bartz, J. A., Zaki, J., et al. (2010). Effects of oxytocin on recollections of maternal care and closeness. *Proceedings of the National Academy of Sciences USA, 107*(50): 21371–21375.

52. Theodosis, D. T. (2002). Oxytocin-secreting neurons: A physiological model of morphological neuronal and glial plasticity in the adult hypothalamus. *Frontiers in Neuroendocrinology, 23*(1): 101–135.

53. Panatier, A., Gentles, S. J., et al. (2006). Activity-dependent synaptic plasticity in the supraoptic nucleus of the rat hypothalamus. *Journal of Physiology, 573*(Pt 3): 711–721.

Chapter 12

1. Rush, A. J., Warden, D., et al. (2009). STAR*D: Revising conventional wisdom. *CNS Drugs, 23*(8): 627–647.

2. de Maat, S. M., Dekker, J., et al. (2007). Relative efficacy of psychotherapy and combined therapy in the treatment of depression: A meta-analysis. *European Psychiatry, 22*(1): 1–8.

3. Rush, et al. (2009). STAR*D.

4. Buchheim, A., Viviani, R., et al. (2012). Changes in prefrontal-limbic function in major depression after 15 months of long-term psychotherapy. *PLoS One, 7*(3): e33745.

5. Ritchey, M., Dolcos, F., et al. (2011). Neural correlates of emotional processing in depression: Changes with cognitive behavioral therapy and predictors of treatment response. *Journal of Psychiatric Research, 45*(5): 577–587.

6. Dichter, G. S., Felder, J. N., et al. (2009). The effects of psychotherapy on neural responses to rewards in major depression. *Biological Psychiatry, 66*(9): 886–897.

7. Martin, S. D., Martin, E., et al. (2001). Brain blood flow changes in depressed patients treated with interpersonal psychotherapy or venlafaxine hydrochloride: Preliminary findings. *Archives of General Psychiatry, 58*(7): 641–648.

8. Goldapple, K., Segal, Z., et al. (2004). Modulation of cortical-limbic pathways in major depression: Treatment-specific effects of cognitive behavior therapy. *Archives of General Psychiatry, 61*(1): 34–41.

9. Farb, N. A., Anderson, A. K., et al. (2010). Minding one's emotions: Mindfulness training alters the neural expression of sadness. *Emotion, 10*(1): 25–33.

10. Karlsson, H., Hirvonen, J., et al. (2010). Research letter: Psychotherapy increases brain serotonin 5-HT1A receptors in patients with major depressive disorder. *Psychological Medicine, 40*(3): 523–528.

11. Lehto, S. M., Tolmunen, T., et al. (2008). Changes in midbrain serotonin transporter availability in atypically depressed subjects after one year of psychotherapy. *Progress in Neuro-Psychopharmacology and Biological Psychiatry, 32*(1): 229–237.

12. Karlsson, et al. (2010). Research letter.

13. Martin, et al. (2001). Brain blood flow changes in depressed patients.

14. Sheline, Y. I., Barch, D. M., et al. (2001). Increased amygdala response to masked emotional faces in depressed subjects resolves with antidepressant treatment: An fMRI study. *Biological Psychiatry, 50*(9): 651–658.

15. Simmons, A. N., Arce, E., et al. (2009). Subchronic SSRI administration reduces insula response during affective anticipation in healthy volunteers. *International Journal of Neuropsychopharmacology, 12*(8): 1009–1020.

16. Morgan, V., Pickens, D., et al. (2005). Amitriptyline reduces rectal pain related activation of the anterior cingulate cortex in patients with irritable bowel syndrome. *Gut, 54*(5): 601–607.

17. Fales, C. L., Barch, D. M., et al. (2009). Antidepressant treatment normalizes hypoactivity in dorsolateral prefrontal cortex during emotional interference processing in major depression. *Journal of Affective Disorders, 112*(1–3): 206–211.

18. El Mansari, M., Sanchez, C., et al. (2005). Effects of acute and long-term administration of escitalopram and citalopram on serotonin neurotransmission: An in vivo electrophysiological study in rat brain. *Neuropsychopharmacology, 30*(7): 1269–1277.

19. Willner, P., Hale, A. S., & Argyropoulos, S. (2005). Dopaminergic mechanism of antidepressant action in depressed patients. *Journal of Affective Disorders, 86*(1): 37–45.

20. Balu, D. T., Hoshaw, B. A., et al. (2008). Differential regulation of central BDNF protein levels by antidepressant and non-antidepressant drug treatments. *Brain Research, 1211*: 37–43.

21. Bessa, J. M., Ferreira, D., et al. (2009). The mood-improving actions of antidepressants do not depend on neurogenesis but are associated with neuronal remodeling. *Molecular Psychiatry, 14*(8): 764–773, 739.

22. Driver, H. S., & Taylor, S. R. (2000). Exercise and sleep. *Sleep Medicine Reviews, 4*(4): 387–402.

23. Knoch, D., Brugger, P., & Regard, M. (2005). Suppressing versus releasing a habit: Frequency-dependent effects of prefrontal transcranial magnetic stimulation. *Cerebral Cortex, 15*(7): 885–887.

24. Cho, S. S., & Strafella, A. P. (2009). rTMS of the left dorsolateral prefrontal cortex modulates dopamine release in the ipsilateral

anterior cingulate cortex and orbitofrontal cortex. *PLoS One, 4*(8): e6725.

25. Nahas, Z., Teneback, C., et al. (2007). Serial vagus nerve stimulation functional MRI in treatment-resistant depression. *Neuropsychopharmacology, 32*(8): 1649–1660.

26. Sackeim, H. A., Prudic, J., et al. (2008). Effects of pulse width and electrode placement on the efficacy and cognitive effects of electroconvulsive therapy. *Brain Stimulation, 1*(2): 71–83.

27. Marano, C. M., Phatak, P., et al. (2007). Increased plasma concentration of brain-derived neurotrophic factor with electroconvulsive therapy: A pilot study in patients with major depression. *Journal of Clinical Psychiatry, 68*(4): 512–517.

28. Merkl, A., Heuser, I., & Bajbouj, M. (2009). Antidepressant electroconvulsive therapy: Mechanism of action, recent advances and limitations. *Experimental Neurology, 219*(1): 20–26.

29. Boggio, P. S., Rigonatti, S. P., et al. (2008). A randomized, double-blind clinical trial on the efficacy of cortical direct current stimulation for the treatment of major depression. *International Journal of Neuropsychopharmacology, 11*(2): 249–254.

30. Mayberg, H. S., Lozano, A. M., et al. (2005). Deep brain stimulation for treatment-resistant depression. *Neuron, 45*(5): 651–660.

Alex Korb, PhD, is a neuroscientist who has studied the brain for over fifteen years, starting with an undergraduate degree in neuroscience from Brown University. He received his PhD in neuroscience from the University of California, Los Angeles, where he wrote his dissertation and numerous scientific articles on depression. He is currently a postdoctoral neuroscience researcher at UCLA in the department of psychiatry. Outside of the lab, he is a scientific consultant for the biotech and pharmaceutical industry, and is head coach of the UCLA Women's Ultimate Frisbee team. He has a wealth of experience in yoga and mindfulness, physical fitness, and even stand-up comedy.

Foreword writer **Daniel J. Siegel, MD**, is executive director of the Mindsight Institute and associate clinical professor of psychiatry at the University of California, Los Angeles School of Medicine. He is author of *The Developing Mind*, *The Mindful Brain*, and other books, and founding editor of the Norton Series on Interpersonal Neurobiology.

For more information or to join the mailing list,
visit alexkorbphd.com.

Real change *is* possible

For more than forty-five years, New Harbinger has published proven-effective self-help books and pioneering workbooks to help readers of all ages and backgrounds improve mental health and well-being, and achieve lasting personal growth. In addition, our spirituality books offer profound guidance for deepening awareness and cultivating healing, self-discovery, and fulfillment.

Founded by psychologist Matthew McKay and Patrick Fanning, New Harbinger is proud to be an independent, employee-owned company. Our books reflect our core values of integrity, innovation, commitment, sustainability, compassion, and trust. Written by leaders in the field and recommended by therapists worldwide, New Harbinger books are practical, accessible, and provide real tools for real change.

newharbingerpublications